Reinventing Asian Populism
Jokowi's Rise, Democracy, and Political Contestation in Indonesia

Policy Studies
an East-West Center series

Series Editors
Dieter Ernst and Marcus Mietzner

Description
Policy Studies presents original research on pressing economic and political policy challenges for governments and industry across Asia, and for the region's relations with the United States. Written for the policy and business communities, academics, journalists, and the informed public, the peer-reviewed publications in this series provide new policy insights and perspectives based on extensive fieldwork and rigorous scholarship.

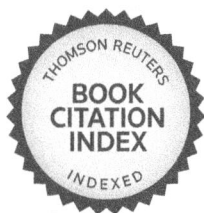

Policy Studies is indexed in the *Web of Science Book Citation Index*. The *Web of Science* is the largest and most comprehensive citation index available.

Notes to Contributors
Submissions may take the form of a proposal or complete manuscript. For more information on the Policy Studies series, please contact the Series Editors.

Editors, Policy Studies
East-West Center
1601 East-West Road
Honolulu, Hawai'i 96848-1601
Tel: 808.944.7197
Publications@EastWestCenter.org
EastWestCenter.org/PolicyStudies

Policy
Studies | 72

Reinventing Asian Populism

Jokowi's Rise, Democracy, and Political Contestation in Indonesia

Marcus Mietzner

Reinventing Asian Populism: Jokowi's Rise, Democracy, and Political Contestation in Indonesia
Marcus Mietzner

ISSN 1547-1349 (print) and 1547-1330 (electronic)
ISBN 978-0-86638-262-5 (print) and 978-0-86638-263-2 (electronic)

Hard copies of all titles, and free electronic copies of most titles, are available from:

Publication Sales Office
East-West Center
1601 East-West Road
Honolulu, Hawai'i 96848-1601
Tel: 808.944.7145
Fax: 808.944.7376
EWCBooks@EastWestCenter.org
EastWestCenter.org/PolicyStudies

In Asia, hard copies of all titles, and electronic copies of select Southeast Asia titles, co-published in Singapore, are available from:

Institute of Southeast Asian Studies
30 Heng Mui Keng Terrace
Pasir Panjang Road, Singapore 119614
publish@iseas.edu.sg
bookshop.iseas.edu.sg

Cover and back cover photographs by Marcus Mietzner.

Contents

List of Acronyms

Gerindra   Great Indonesia Movement Party
(Partai Gerakan Indonesia Raya)

Golkar   Party of the Functional Groups
(Partai Golongan Karya)

Hanura   People's Conscience Party
(Partai Hati Nurani Rakyat)

HKTI   Indonesian Farmers' Harmony Association
(Himpunan Kerukunan Tani Indonesia)

KPK   Corruption Eradication Commission
(Komisi Pemberantasan Korupsi)

KPU   General Elections Commission
(Komisi Pemilihan Umum)

Nasdem   Party of National Democrats
(Partai Nasional Demokrat)

PAN   National Mandate Party (Partai Amanat Nasional)

PD   Democratic Party (Partai Demokrat)

PDI	Indonesian Democratic Party (Partai Demokrasi Indonesia)
PDIP	Indonesian Democratic Party of Struggle (Partai Demokrasi Indonesia Perjuangan)
PKB	National Awakening Party (Partai Kebangkitan Bangsa)
PKPI	Party of Indonesian Justice and Unity (Partai Keadilan dan Persatuan Indonesia)
PKS	Prosperous Justice Party (Partai Keadilan Sejahtera)
PPP	United Development Party (Partai Persatuan Pembangunan)

Executive Summary

In the last two decades, populists around the world have celebrated a renaissance. As the role of political parties declines, and globalization creates socioeconomic uncertainties that unsettle anxious electorates, anti-establishment figures or movements have found it easy to attract support. Whether Hugo Chavez in Venezuela, Thaksin Shinawatra in Thailand, Narendra Modi in India, or Alexis Tsipras in Greece, populists have been able to mobilize voters by attacking a supposedly collective enemy (mostly, domestic or foreign forces accused of exploiting the country's economic resources) and by appealing to the poor as their main constituency. In some cases, populists have been so successful at the ballot box that established political forces resorted to violence to try removing them—as evidenced by the failed coup against Chavez in 2002, and the military overthrows of Thaksin in 2006 and of his sister, Yingluck, in 2014.

Quite unusually, the 2014 presidential election in Indonesia was a contest *between* two populists, albeit of a very different kind. Prabowo Subianto, the former son-in-law of the country's long-time autocrat Suharto, followed almost all the guidelines of classic textbook populism: he condemned the existing polity as broken and beyond repair; he attacked foreign companies for extracting Indonesia's natural wealth without proper compensation; he portrayed

Jokowi didn't promise to revamp the political system—he offered change within the framework of the democratic status quo

the domestic elites as cronies of those foreign parasites; he appealed primarily to the poor, uneducated, and rural population for support; and he pursued an inherently anti-democratic agenda, promising tougher leadership instead of lengthy, multilayered deliberations.

By contrast, his opponent, Jakarta governor Joko Widodo ("Jokowi"), introduced a new form of populism that differed from the standard version in several ways. First, Jokowi did not promise to completely revamp the political system—he offered change within the framework of the democratic status quo. Second, he did not target any particular actor or group as an enemy, instead presenting himself as highly inclusivist. And third, he refrained from anti-foreign rhetoric to shore up support. As a substitute, he focused on improved public service delivery as the core element of his platform, and relied on his man-of-the-people image to bind ordinary voters to his cause. Successes in the areas of health and education reform, plus a carefully cultivated down-to-earth attitude, had delivered Jokowi electoral victories and strong approval ratings in the city of Solo, where he had been mayor, and in Jakarta. Thus, Jokowi pitched his technocratic, intra-systemic populism against Prabowo's ultra-nationalist, confrontational populism.

This study explores the dynamics of the electoral contest between Prabowo and Jokowi, and analyzes what they tell us about the conditions under which populist campaigns are launched and succeed or fail. It shows that Prabowo's classic populist campaign ultimately collapsed because, unlike many other polities in which successful populist challenges were launched, Indonesia's post-Suharto democracy was not in a state of acute, life-threatening crisis. While there was simmering discontent, support for democracy remained high among the electorate; economic conditions were stable; and the majority of voters, in general, did not desire regime change. In addition, Prabowo, who originated from a wealthy, established political family, found it difficult to gain credibility among Indonesia's poor, especially when confronted with Jokowi's biography of genuinely humble beginnings.

The victory of Jokowi's technocratic populism, then, reflected the mood of Indonesia's electorate 16 years after the end of authoritarianism. There was frustration about the ineffectiveness of service delivery, and about the corruption in established political parties and institutions. At the same time, however, the majority of voters enjoyed the extensive democratic rights they had been given since Suharto's fall, and therefore opposed notions of returning to autocratic rule. Jokowi's pragmatic populism, which prioritized improvements to day-to-day services over grand political visions, and which promised to maintain democracy, captured this mood perfectly. In other words, what most Indonesian voters wanted was not full-blown populism à la Chavez—they wanted some form of populism-lite.

But the aftermath of Jokowi's election also demonstrated the limitations of his specific populism as a method of governance. Being inclusive, nonconfrontational, and supportive of the democratic status quo, Jokowi made himself vulnerable to influence meddling by oligarchs, party leaders, and other patronage-driven actors. Unlike Prabowo, who had

Jokowi's pragmatic populism prioritized service improvements over grand political visions

planned to reshape the political system to suit his interests, Jokowi had no intention of radically changing the polity. This also meant that he allowed the forces of the establishment, whether they were in opposition or part of the coalition that had nominated him, to aggressively (and successfully) defend their interests. In particular, Jokowi proved reluctant to reject requests from Megawati Sukarnoputri, the former president and chairperson of his party, and Surya Paloh, an oligarch who had provided him with assistance during his campaign.

Thus, while extraordinarily effective as an electoral strategy, Jokowi's technocratic and inclusive populism ran into serious problems the moment he assumed the presidency. In the first months of his term, he often looked helpless when confronted with the vested interests present in parliament, his own coalition, and the government apparatus. It took a severe political crisis in January 2015—triggered by Megawati's insistence that Jokowi appoint her corrupt former adjutant as police chief—to convince the president that he needed to start emancipating himself. He cancelled the appointment of Megawati's protégée as police chief, began to balance opposition and government parties in a way that benefited him, and pushed a budget through parliament that supported the key components of his technocratic agenda. Hence, Jokowi's rule, and the concept of technocratic populism upon which it was based, began to stabilize somewhat. Nevertheless, given the nonconfrontational nature of this concept, it is unlikely that Jokowi plans to completely cut his ties to the establishment.

This monograph's discussion of the 2014 competition between two Indonesian populists also has important implications for the debate on the state of post-Suharto democracy. On the one hand, Jokowi's victory seems to provide strong evidence to support a pluralist approach to analyzing Indonesian democracy (according to which reformist and conservative forces incessantly compete, and no force has achieved complete domination over the other). On the other hand, scholars who believe that the post-authoritarian polity is under oligarchic control feel that the campaign and its aftermath have strengthened their case. They particularly point to Jokowi's apparent inability to make decisions without external elite intrusion. While acknowledging the validity of the oligarchic theorists' observations, this issue locates the Jokowi campaign and presidency firmly within a pluralist interpretation of Indonesian politics.

Reinventing Asian Populism
Jokowi's Rise, Democracy, and Political Contestation in Indonesia

Introduction

The inauguration of Joko Widodo, or "Jokowi," as Indonesia's seventh president on October 20, 2014, marked a set of milestones for the country's young democracy. Jokowi became the first president not to originate from one of Indonesia's traditional power networks: that is, political families, the military, the bureaucracy, or Muslim mass organizations. He was also the first to have been born after Indonesia obtained its sovereignty from the Netherlands in late 1949, with all other presidents before him born either during colonial rule or at the time of the guerrilla war against the Dutch (1945–1949). Moreover, he was the first head of state to have assumed office from a position in local government, providing evidence that decentralization had brought a new generation of political leaders to the fore. Finally, Jokowi's ascension to power constituted the first time a directly elected president had taken over from another directly elected head of state, pointing to the increasing institutionalization of elections as the primary mechanism of power transfers. Between the 1940s and the early 2000s, by contrast, Indonesian presidents had received the insignia of power through elite consensus (Sukarno), military intervention (Suharto), resignation of the incumbent (Habibie), indirect elections (Abdurrahman Wahid), or controversial impeachment proceedings (Megawati Sukarnoputri).

Jokowi's rise to the presidency was also remarkable because it came after the most divisive election in Indonesian history. In the presidential ballot in July 2014, Jokowi defeated Prabowo Subianto, who had launched a major populist challenge against Indonesia's democratic polity. While Prabowo was the epitome of an elite politician—he was a multimillionaire, came from an aristocratic family, had served as one of Suharto's top generals, and was once his son-in-law—his campaign copied that of other pro-poor, Third World populists. Proclaiming that the rich and powerful were looting Indonesia's natural resources in collaboration with foreign powers, Prabowo appealed mainly to the rural lower classes to hand him a mandate to clean up the country. As is often

Prabowo's pro-poor appeal mixed with clearly authoritarian overtones

the case with conventional populists, his pro-poor appeal mixed with clearly authoritarian overtones. He promised a return to the original version of the 1945 constitution, potentially rolling back the constitutional amendments instituted between 1998 and 2002. If implemented, this initiative would have led to the recentralization of presidential powers and the abolition of direct elections at all levels of executive government, and would have allowed Prabowo to restore many elements of Suharto's authoritarian rule. While Prabowo lost the election against Jokowi, he gathered almost 47 percent of the votes, highlighting the fact that radically populist ideas had fallen on fertile ground in Indonesia.

Indeed, even Jokowi's victory was a triumph of populism, albeit of a very different kind. Like Prabowo, Jokowi embodied widespread disillusionment with the 10-year rule of Susilo Bambang Yudhoyono (2004–2014). He was critical of the unabated, endemic corruption, demanded better governance and public services for the lower classes, and his humble origins as a small-town carpenter stood in stark contrast to the pretentiousness of Jakarta elite politics. But unlike Prabowo's belligerent rhetoric, the soft-spoken Jokowi did not attack the rich or foreign powers; he did not portray Indonesia's democratic system as being in decay; and he did not present a neo-authoritarian alternative to the status quo. Rather, he offered his humility, politeness, and hard work ethics as a counternarrative to the arrogance, hostility, and self-indulgence of the political establishment, without openly confronting it. Clearly, Jokowi's efficiency-oriented, technocratic populism was very different from classic concepts of populism in the developing world: it was inclusive rather than focused on the exclusion of an identified enemy; it was nationalist, but used none of the anti-foreign rhetoric so many Asian or Latin American populists rely on; and it suggested improvements to the existing polity instead of calling for its replacement. It seemed, then, that Jokowi's populism presented something new—not only for Indonesia, but also for Asia and the rest of the developing world.

Of course, the emergence of Jokowi's new populism coincided with the rise and fall of other populists around Asia. In India, the Hindu nationalist Narendra Modi won the April and May 2014 parliamentary elections on the back of a more classic populist approach. He strongly criticized the political class and wasn't shy about courting the anti-Muslim vote (Varshney 2014). While many observers compared Modi to Jokowi (like him, Modi had become popular as head of a local administration),[1] the characters of the two men couldn't have been more different. For example, one of Jokowi's ideological cornerstones was religious inclusivism. Similarly, Jokowi was very different from the other Asian populist who made headlines in 2014: Thailand's Thaksin Shinawatra, whose sister was removed from power in May by a network of royalist, bureaucratic, and military interests. Thaksin's populism—which had pitched poor voters in the North and Northeast of the country against Bangkok's powerful elite—had been extraordinarily successful at the ballot box, but had provoked constant counterreactions by his opponents (Kosuke and Phongpaichit 2009). As a result, Thai politics have been paralyzed since the mid-2000s, with the 2006 and 2014 military coups trying to keep Thaksin and his relatives away from power. Like Modi, Thaksin was a classic populist in that he combined his appeal to one constituency with attacks on another. And like other populists in developing countries, Thaksin acquired an increasingly autocratic attitude, triggering protests that eventually led to his fall.

How, then, does Jokowi's technocratic populism fit into the broader context of populism in Asia and beyond? Is it a truly new phenomenon, or is it an adaptation and redevelopment of existing concepts of populism? In order to approach such questions effectively, we first have to understand the causes for Jokowi's rise, the way he prevailed over his other populist challenger, and what that tells us about his strategic approach and conceptual thinking. It is equally important to examine how Jokowi's ascent sits with conventional interpretations of Indonesian politics after 1998. Some of these accounts have described post-Suharto Indonesia as being under the control of oligarchs and/or political party cartels, with elections only held to mask the dominance of these elites (Hadiz and Robison 2014, Slater and Simmons 2013). According to the neo-Marxist versions of these critiques, Indonesia's democratic institutions have been hijacked by the rich and well-connected, making it impossible for outsiders to come to power. Do Jokowi's electoral victory and observations of his first few months in office contradict such analyses, or is Jokowi simply a puppet of oligarchs and other elite actors? These questions will have to be explored in order to contextualize Jokowi's rise within the more general debate of populism in the developing world.

Is Jokowi simply a puppet of oligarchs and other elite actors, as many critics say?

This study proceeds in nine analytical steps. The first section introduces common interpretations of Indonesian politics since 1998, many of which have focused on the power of oligarchs and cartels. The second section discusses the decade-long rule of Yudhoyono, which provided the context that made a populist challenge to Indonesian democracy possible. The third segment describes Prabowo's classic, confrontational populism, which borrowed from textbook populist campaigns around the world. Subsequently, the fourth part explains the main elements of Jokowi's populist counterconcept, which emphasized inclusivism, technocratic competence, and moderation. The fifth section describes Jokowi's difficult path to the presidential nomination of his party, while the sixth and seventh segments discuss the parliamentary election in April, as well as the ensuing presidential campaign. In combination, these sections highlight the reasons for his success, and also a number of shortcomings that almost cost him the election. The eighth section focuses on the aftermath of the election and Jokowi's attempts to form a workable government, a process that demonstrated the continued influence of Indonesia's old political forces. Finally, the conclusion shows that Jokowi's rise—compromises with established elites notwithstanding—points to the emergence of a new type of nonbelligerent, technocratic populism that necessitates some conceptual rethinking of existing approaches to both Indonesian politics and to the study of populism.

Oligarchs and Cartels? Interpretations of Indonesia's Post-1998 Democracy

Jokowi's rise to national prominence occurred at a time when most scholars of Indonesian politics believed that the grip of oligarchic and predatory elites on the country's political and economic institutions was tightening. In other words, the prospect that a small-town administrator with few financial resources and political connections would emerge as Indonesia's next leader was seen as highly unlikely. In broad terms, the study of Indonesian politics from the late 1990s to the mid-2010s can be divided into three major schools of thought. First, there is a stream that has focused on the growing power of oligarchs in politics, the economy, and society; second, a group of scholars who have applied the cartel party theory to Indonesia, highlighting that its parties are increasingly colluding among each other to jointly exploit the resources of the state; and third, a "pluralist" school that has viewed post-Suharto Indonesia as an arena of ongoing contestation between oligarchic, cartelistic, and similarly predatory forces on the one hand and pro-reform groups and conventional politicians on the other. While there have been stark differences between these camps, they have generally agreed that the quality of Indonesian democracy declined gradually during Yudhoyono's second term.

To begin with, the proponents of the oligarchy theory in Indonesia see the post-1998 polity in the claws of a small class of massively wealthy individuals, assisted by their cronies and political fixers. However, the authors proposing such an interpretation are themselves divided into two groups. One camp draws from neo-Marxist thought, portraying Indonesia's entire political, social, and economic infrastructure as "a system of power relations that enables the concentration of wealth and authority and its collective defense" (Hadiz and Robison 2014, 35). In this system, democratic institutions and procedures (such as parties and elections) necessarily serve the interests of capital accumulation and its drivers, the oligarchs. Indeed, for the main proponents of this theory, Vedi R. Hadiz and Richard Robison, Indonesia is part of a global system that operates based on the same dynamics. The other stream within the broader oligarchy paradigm is represented by Jeffrey Winters's more actor-oriented approach. For him, oligarchs "are actors who command and control massive concentrations of material resources that can be deployed to defend or enhance their personal wealth and exclusive social position" (Winters 2011, 6). While describing the current post-Suharto polity as an "untamed ruling oligarchy" (Winters 2011, 181), Winters has a more procedural view of power relations than Hadiz and Robison. Concretely, Winters developed a typology of different oligarchic regime forms, according to which countries can move between categories if the influence of oligarchs rises or falls.

For most oligarchy theorists, the power of wealthy actors and their political associates in Indonesia is so strong that no substantial reform can occur without oligarchic approval. For Hadiz and Robison, for example, the efforts of reformist politicians, NGOs (nongovernmental organizations), and other civil society forces will remain meaningless as long as the overall politico-economic framework remains in place. Ascribing no "larger transformative significance" to counter-oligarchic actors, they believe that "incremental demands for reform by individuals or groups can only be piecemeal" (Hadiz and Robison 2014, 54). This also implies that the rise of a politician to the presidency is only possible if oligarchs and their proxies in the political institutions endorse or at least tolerate it. In fact, for Hadiz and Robison, change cannot come through elections within the existing regime—the latter just reproduce the incumbent power arrangements. Therefore, Hadiz and Robison (2014, 54) demand nothing less than "the disintegration of the old order and its social underpinnings and the forging of a new social order with its political forces." Winters (2013, 32), for his part, views Indonesia's anti-oligarchic forces as too weak and fragmented to make a significant difference, although he acknowledges that they are not "irrelevant." For him, as for Hadiz and Robison, it appears currently unthinkable that a politician can climb to the apex of Indonesian political power without being sponsored by rich elites.

The second main school in interpreting the patterns of Indonesia's post-Suharto democracy is centered on the cartelization model. The cartel party paradigm was developed in the mid-1990s by Richard Katz and Peter Mair (1995, 1996), proposing that parties in Western Europe and other mature democracies were collaborating with rather than competing against each other. In doing so, Katz and Mair contended, parties focused on gaining access to state resources, primarily through significant public funding for their treasuries. As parties ceased to oppose each other in the interest of plundering the state, elections turned into meaningless charades and were only upheld to create the impression of competition (Katz and Mair 2009, 2012). In 2004, Dan Slater was the first to apply Katz's and Mair's model to the Indonesian case, arguing that a large party cartel had formed that distributed the state's patronage resources among its members (Slater 2004). The broad-based, inclusivist "rainbow" coalitions under both Megawati Sukarnoputri (2001–2004) and Yudhoyono served as evidence for this claim, and many Indonesian observers agreed (Ambardi 2008, 2009). Elections, Slater argued, merely led to the reconstitution of the same cartel in a slightly different configuration, robbing voters of the opportunity to punish incumbents and vote in alternative leaders. As a result, accountability mechanisms have broken down, with the electorate unable to hold incumbent state officials responsible for their actions (or the lack thereof). In the early 2010s, Slater developed the cartel theory further, now increasingly preferring the term "promiscuous powersharing" (Slater and Simmons 2013).

For the most part, cartelization scholars have described the possibility of a noncartel force to emerge and break up the monopoly of the ruling Indonesian party alliance as small but not completely implausible. Indeed, in contrast to most oligarchy theorists, Slater and other proponents of the cartel paradigm have put much more emphasis on political agency than on structural inevitability. In their view, changes in the composition of coalitions (such as the exclusion of a significant number of parties from government, for instance) can lead to

Cartelization scholars view elections as reshufflings of the same cartel in slightly different configurations

different outcomes as far as the quality of accountability is concerned. Nevertheless, in assessing the likelihood of political scenarios outside of the continuation of cartelist rule, Slater and others have focused more on anti-democratic alternatives than on the probability of a re-formist challenger to arise (let alone to succeed). Writing in 2013, Slater and Simmons (2013, 25) predicted that "the biggest danger for democratic stability is that oligarchic exclusion will lead [Indonesian voters] to pursue populist inclusion, unintentionally empowering a strongman with little tolerance for democratic constraints." Taking into account the trend of opinion polling in the early 2010s, Slater and Simmons identified Prabowo Subianto as the most likely candi-date for launching such a populist challenge. Unsurprisingly, given the political context at that time, they did not consider the prospect of an alternative, pro-democracy populist to challenge the status quo without promising to overthrow it.

In contrast to the oligarchic and cartelist schools, the "pluralists" suggest that post-authoritarian Indonesia has seen an incessant con-test between predatory and counter-oligarchic forces. This contest takes place not only between politico-economic elites and civil society groups, but also between conservative and reformist elements within the elite itself. Thus, the pluralists assert that Winters's notion of a "ruling" oligarchy and Slater's reference to "all-encompassing" cartels (Slater 2011) inadvertently distract from the intricacy of Indonesia's multilayered politics. As Edward Aspinall (2014c, 135) put it: "We have become overused to viewing Indonesia as a site

A third school—the pluralists—believe it's possible for an outsider to penetrate the top echelons of power

of political domination; it remains equally a place of contestation—in the contentious politics of street protests and social movements that have become central to political life, and in the perpetual frictions that occur between oligarchic, popular, and other interests within are-nas like parliaments, parties, and electoral politics." Pluralists accept that oligarchic forces are powerful, but maintain that the latter don't *rule* Indonesia; and while they agree that there are cartelist tenden-cies within parties, pluralists do not find that political and ideologi-cal struggles have ceased as a result (Liddle 2014; Mietzner 2013). Indeed, "that these struggles are complex, and take place in contra-dictory and fragmented ways, involving ever-shifting political coali-tions and conflicts, reflects the complexity of Indonesian democracy and the kaleidoscopic patterns of social interest that underpin it" (Aspinall 2014c, 135).

Among the three dominant schools in the study of Indonesian politics, the pluralists have been most receptive to the possibility of democratic outsiders penetrating the top echelons of power. For example, whereas oligarchy theorists dismissed Indonesia's decentralization process as a pathway to more predatory rent-seeking (Hadiz 2010), pluralists identified it as a channel through which reformist politicians could gain influence—despite the continued strength of elite networks (Mietzner 2005; Aspinall 2010). In describing the patterns of political conflict in Indonesia, pluralists have insisted on the basic point that "elite forces often come out on top—but not always. In a not insignificant number of cases, non-elite groups have prevailed" (Mietzner 2013, 29). For pluralists, though, occasional victories of reformers do not point to their long-term ascendancy, just as frequent oligarchic triumphs do not mean permanent oligarchic domination. Nevertheless, even pluralist scholars agreed with their oligarchic and cartelist counterparts that by the early 2010s, pro-democracy forces faced an increasingly difficult struggle. Anti-reformist elites were consolidating during Yudhoyono's second term, launching attempts to roll back democratic achievements (Tomsa 2010; Fealy 2011; Mietzner 2012a). Opinion polls on the most likely candidates for Yudhoyono's succession pointed to the continued popularity of old establishment figures, such as Prabowo or Megawati, who still chaired the nationalist Indonesian Democratic Party of Struggle (Partai Demokrasi Indonesia Perjuangan, PDIP). Thus, even from a pluralist perspective, there was little in the early 2010s to suggest that the 2014 presidential elections would see the meteoric rise of a democratic populist with a nonelite background.

Yudhoyono's Democracy: Consolidation and Stagnation

In developing their approaches to Indonesian politics, all three schools of thought have focused heavily on Yudhoyono's presidency between 2004 and 2014. Indeed, despite their different analytical lenses, all three paradigms have found much material in Yudhoyono's rule to back up their respective stances. This should not come as a surprise. Like no other president before him, Yudhoyono was able to synthesize a vast array of sociopolitical interests into an all-inclusive agenda—an agenda that led him to two landslide electoral victories, but also attracted accusations of shallowness. Espousing polite rhetoric and an overall conservative demeanor, Yudhoyono appealed to a wide spectrum: political reformers and leftovers of the New Order, supporters of religious pluralism and advocates of a stronger role for Islam in state affairs, ideological moderates and radicals, free-market liberals and economic protectionists, and internationalists and ultra-nationalists. As the great integrationist of Indonesian politics, Yudhoyono personified the thirst of many citizens for politico-ideological depolarization after six tumultuous years of democratic transition between 1998 and 2004. Yudhoyono put much pride in his catchall inclusivism, saying that the role of a president is to "create balance" between competing sociopolitical forces.[2] The price for Yudhoyono's approach was high, however, both for him personally and for the country. At the end of his decade in power, most Indonesians still did not know what—if anything—Yudhoyono stood for; and Indonesia, while politically and economically stable, was frequently criticized as a stagnating polity on autopilot.

Looking at Indonesia from afar, and adopting a minimalist view of effective democratic consolidation, Yudhoyono's presidency appeared like an outstanding success. Under Yudhoyono, democracy was preserved, while Indonesia was spared large-scale political or communal violence for a decade—not a small feat for a country with a long history of bloody conflict, and whose single pre-1998 experiment with democracy had been aborted after only seven years in 1957 (Feith 1962). Moreover, Yudhoyono ended the 30-year separatist insurgency in Aceh through a political settlement, proving to his hard-line critics that rebellions can be resolved with negotiations rather than by military force (Aspinall 2009; Morfit 2007). In the Yudhoyono decade, the relationship between the executive, the legislature, and the judiciary was functional, without any major crisis. Significantly, civil society remained strong and often provided a counterweight to the formal political arena, while the media was largely free. Economically, Yudhoyono's presidency recorded continuously high GDP growth rates of between 5 percent and 6 percent per annum; poverty and unemployment numbers declined; the country became a lower middle-income country and joined the exclusive club of one-trillion-dollar economies; and the Human Development Index improved (Hill 2014). On the international stage, Yudhoyono became a respected statesman (Reid 2012), popular both in the West (where he was seen as the head of a model Muslim democracy) and in countries such as China and Russia (where Indonesia's refusal to formally align with the West was appreciated). Thus, Yudhoyono's much-displayed satisfaction with himself seemed well-deserved.

But behind the façade of stability and success, Yudhoyono left many problems unresolved. In fact, Aspinall (2010) argued that the stability of Yudhoyono's rule and the concurrent persistence of anti-democratic habits were inseparably linked. From this perspective, it was Yudhoyono's embrace of conservative groups (mostly oligarchic, bureaucratic, military, and religious elites) and their patronage-soaked practices that guaranteed the solidity of Indonesian democracy—which, in turn, created space for reformist forces too. In no other area was this ambivalence more pronounced than in the fight against corruption. Despite portraying himself as an anti-corruption crusader, Yudhoyono's commitment to this cause was questionable at best. Indeed, he allowed his Democratic Party (Partai Demokrat, PD) and his cabinet to develop into hotbeds of corruption and patronage. At the end of his rule, a host of PD politicians were either in prison or indicted for corruption (including the former chairman, the treasurer, two ministers, and several legislators). Furthermore, some corruption suspects implicated Yudhoyono's son, Edhie Baskoro Yudhoyono, the PD secretary-general.[3] Beyond PD, the chairpersons of two of Yudhoyono's coalition parties were imprisoned or indicted as well. Hence, although Indonesia's ranking in Transparency International's Corruption Perceptions Index improved during Yudhoyono's rule (from 133rd in 2004 to 107th in 2014), this was largely due to the increased number of arrests (i.e., the perception of better enforcement), rather than a real decline in the level of political corruption.

Yudhoyono's unwillingness to seriously tackle Indonesia's endemic corruption found its parallels in other policy areas. As a matter of fact, in his 10 years as president, Yudhoyono did not launch a single

> *Yudhoyono failed to tackle Indonesia's corruption or launch any reforms of democratic governance*

structural reform project in the field of democratic governance. Even when other institutions proposed reform initiatives, Yudhoyono tended to obstruct, delay, or dilute them. For instance, when parliament submitted a bill in 2010 that would have created an independent body in charge of senior bureaucratic appointments, Yudhoyono watered the concept down to such an extent that the eventually legislated agency was widely seen as a paper tiger (Mietzner 2014a). Caving in to opposition from his leading bureaucrats, Yudhoyono terminated the most meaningful post-Suharto attempt at administrative reform—despite having defined the reorganization of the bureaucracy as his top priority in 2009.[4] In the same vein, Yudhoyono demonstrated very little interest in military reform, an area in which he had gained prominence as a reform-minded officer under Suharto's rule. The Armed Forces Act, which regulates the governance of the armed forces, had been passed in the dying days of the Megawati presidency in 2004—and Yudhoyono did not make any revisions to it in his decade in office (Lorenz 2013). In short, although he exercised robust civilian control over the armed forces, Yudhoyono introduced no reforms that could have institutionalized this oversight for his successor.

While Yudhoyono was reluctant to support, let alone initiate, political reform, he held an ambiguous attitude toward political institutions that had been established shortly before his presidency. To be sure, he oversaw the technical operationalization of these new bodies, consolidating them in the process. But on at least three occasions, he felt tempted to roll back key reforms launched under Megawati. The first related to the widely respected Constitutional Court, created in 2003 (Butt 2006). Yudhoyono generally honored its verdicts, but he often felt a deep dismay about them. In 2013, using a crisis in the court, he issued a decree that would have imposed stronger external control over its judges. His initiative failed, however, because of opposition from parliament. Second, Yudhoyono occasionally encouraged his subordinates to try to weaken the Corruption Eradication Commission (Komisi Pemberantasan Korupsi, KPK). In 2009, for example, the government and parliament discussed removing the KPK's wiretapping and prosecution powers, both indispensable instruments for the agency. Yudhoyono, who believed that the KPK was too powerful,[5] only backtracked after a strong public backlash. Finally, in 2012, Yudhoyono allowed his minister of the interior to propose abolishing direct local elections—a landmark reform legislated under Megawati that prompted Freedom House to upgrade Indonesia from "partly free" to "free" in 2006 (Freedom House 2006). Once again, Yudhoyono relented only after he sensed solid opposition to his move. Hence, while Yudhoyono cooperated with the democratic institutions founded before he took office, his commitment to their long-term endurance and further deepening was fragile.

Under Yudhoyono, Indonesia also recorded an erosion in the protection of religious minority rights. Fearful that alienating conservative Muslim groups would reduce his popularity, Yudhoyono stood by as militant Islamists began to attack non-Muslim, Ahmadi, and Shiite constituencies from the mid-2000s onward. The Setara Institute, a group advocating for religious tolerance, recorded 91 cases of such attacks in 2007, 257 cases in 2008, 181 in 2009, 216 in 2010, 242 in 2011, 264 in 2012, and 220 in 2013 (Harsono 2014). In the name of freedom of expression and maintaining "balance" between conservative Islamists and activists defending the minorities,[6] Yudhoyono refused to unequivocally criminalize the perpetrators. The trend of increasing violence against religious minorities reduced Indo-

> *Protection of religious minorities eroded under Yudhoyono and increasing violence damaged Indonesia's democratic quality*

nesia's democratic quality at home and damaged its reputation abroad. Freedom House, for example, downgraded Indonesia in 2014 from "free" to "partly free." While this was done in reaction to the passing of a law that could potentially restrict the activities of NGOs, Freedom House also highlighted that "the central government has often failed to respond to religious intolerance in recent years, and societal discrimination has increased" (Freedom House 2014). Thus, according to Freedom House, Indonesia in 2014 was at the same level of democratic quality as it was in 2004, when Yudhoyono took office. Given the absence of meaningful reform initiatives under Yudhoyono, it is hard to argue with this assessment.

But the general sense of stagnation surrounding Yudhoyono's rule had not only political causes, but also economic ones. As in the case of Yudhoyono's political record, a closer look behind the frontage of his economic success revealed major shortcomings. Chief among them was Indonesia's continued reliance on commodities. Profiting from the global commodity boom between the early 2000s and early 2010s, Indonesia attracted capital-intensive investments in natural resource extraction. While these investments drove up GDP growth, they did not create enough jobs to absorb the millions of young people entering the labor market each year. Indeed, the labor-intensive manufacturing sector declined under Yudhoyono, from constituting 28 percent of total GDP in 2004 to a level of 24 percent at the end of his term (World Bank 2014a). As a result, the percentage of Indonesians trapped in jobs in the informal sector remained stagnant under Yudhoyono—it was 59.4 percent when he left office (BPS 2014, 44). And while official poverty numbers declined, 43 percent of Indonesians still lived on less than US$2 a day as Yudhoyono's rule drew to a close (World Bank 2014b). By contrast, the country had the fastest growth rate of millionaires in Asia, with its numbers tripling to 100,000 between 2010 and 2015.[7]

Poorer Indonesians felt that healthy GDP growth did not benefit them

This trend was also reflected in record levels of inequality: Indonesia's Gini index, which measures income distribution, rose from 0.37 in 2009 to 0.41 in 2011.[8] Accordingly, many poorer Indonesians felt that the healthy GDP growth did not benefit them—in the words of *The Economist*, "the rich are getting richer much more rapidly than the poor are."[9]

Yudhoyono also failed to significantly advance the development of Indonesia's infrastructure, leaving behind a network of debilitated roads, railways, and power plants. Under his rule, Indonesia spent only around 4 percent of GDP on infrastructure—half of what China and India allocated in those periods, and half of what Suharto used to expend during the New Order regime (Oberman et al. 2012, 23–24; McVey 2013, 20). Total spending on health also remained dismally low: 3 percent of GDP in 2012, compared to China's 5.4 percent (World Bank 2014c). The situation in education was similar: Indonesia's expenditure on education was 3.6 percent of GDP in 2012, compared to Brazil's 5.8 percent (World Bank 2014d). What's more, while capital and social spending was low under Yudhoyono, he maintained the huge fuel and electricity subsidies that mostly benefited the middle class. In 2014, these subsidies consumed a whopping US$29 billion, or 19 percent of the government's total budget (Howes and Davies 2014). Despite Yudhoyono's publicly expressed awareness that these subsidies were nonsensical from an economic and developmental perspective, he lacked the political courage to abolish them. As a result, the subsidies were at an all-time high at the end of his rule.

Most observers, and Yudhoyono himself, have explained his reluctance to push for major political and economic change by pointing to the composition of his government coalition. As indicated above, Yudhoyono—like Megawati—opted to build an oversized presidential coalition, i.e., to include more parties in his cabinet than would be required for an absolute majority in the legislature (Slater and Simmons 2013). Although this protected him from potential impeachment moves by parliament (he explicitly mentioned Wahid's dismissal by the legislature as the reason for creating a "rainbow" coalition[10]), it also made decision making exceedingly difficult (Sherlock 2015). With a diverse range of parties exploiting their ministries as sources of patronage, policy coordination across departments was close to impossible. Yudhoyono, for his part, credited himself for not exercising "authoritarian" control over this quasi-anarchic coalition of government parties. Stating that the times of autarchic presidential leadership were over, Yudhoyono believed that he offered a laudable model of democratic management by moderating government business rather than directing it (Yudhoyono 2014). The lack of uncompromising presidential directives, in Yudhoyono's view, was a necessary by-product of democratization, rather than an indication of missing courage or determination. Of course, Yudhoyono's defense of his hesitant leadership style, as laid out in his 2014 book, appeared to some more like a post-factum rationalization of his personal fondness for risk-aversion, rather than a practitioner's guide for successful governance (Fealy 2015).

Indeed, Indonesians not only grew weary of the Yudhoyono presidency because of its political and economic record, but they also came to resent the president's increasingly wooden personality. Harboring a predilection for ceremonies since childhood, Yudhoyono found more and more pleasure in the protocol and rituals attached to his office, both at home and abroad. Especially after his compelling reelection in 2009, Yudhoyono showed much less interest in the minutiae of governance than in presidential pageantry. According to aides, he became less tolerant of criticism, and he began to lecture rather than listen to his conversation partners, including ministers and other political notables (Fealy 2015). Sometime in his second term, Yudhoyono drastically reduced the frequency of his media interviews. Instead, he conducted "dialogues" with his press secretary, which were recorded and uploaded on YouTube. In addition, he conveyed messages to the electorate through Facebook and Twitter, insulating him from the potentiality of critical questions from journalists. At the end of his term, then, Yudhoyono appeared aloof and self-indulgent, satisfied with his achievements and unwilling to hear any views that could smear them. He traveled the world to collect prizes, awards, and honorary doctorates, some of which had been solicited by a special team located in the presidential office. In short, Yudhoyono became the embodiment of the complacent stagnation that commentators had identified in both the political and economic arenas.

The twin legacies of Yudhoyono's presidency—widely praised stability and much-criticized stagnation at the same time—were reflected in the opinion polls during his second term. On the one hand, Yudhoyono's personal approval ratings dropped dramatically. From 75 percent in November 2009, his ratings declined to 47 percent in June 2011 and 30 percent in May 2013. His numbers only recovered somewhat in 2014, when voters paid more attention to the candidates for Yudhoyono's succession than to his lame-duck presidency.[11] On the other hand, the electorate continued to express satisfaction with the way democracy functioned in Indonesia. In October 2013, as Yudhoyono entered his final year, 53 percent of Indonesians stated in an opinion poll that they were satisfied with Indonesia's democracy, while 38 percent were dissatisfied (SMRC 2014c). Thus, Indonesian voters' assessment of Yudhoyono's legacy was as ambiguous as that legacy itself: their rejection of Yudhoyono's performance in his second term was profound, calling for something—and someone—fundamentally different; at the same time, the majority of citizens, it seemed, wanted Yudhoyono's successor to remain within the corridor of the existing democratic polity. This multilayered mood in the electorate, dispensing both pro– and anti–status quo messages, formed the backdrop against which the candidates for Yudhoyono's succession emerged and positioned themselves.

Prabowo's Populist Challenge

The calcification of democracy during Yudhoyono's rule created fertile ground for an anti-establishment challenger to claim the presidency in 2014. As mentioned above, Slater and Simmons warned of the possible rise of a populist, anti-democratic figure, and they pointed to Prabowo as the most likely candidate for this role. And indeed, Prabowo took the lead in presidential opinion polls early in Yudhoyono's second term. In a poll taken in October 2011, he topped the list of the most popular nominees for the presidency, attracting 28 percent support.[12] For much of 2011 and 2012, Prabowo maintained his lead, only sometimes coming second to Megawati—who wasn't considered a serious candidate as she had lost two previous presidential races against Yudhoyono and was deeply unpopular outside of her loyalist, secular-nationalist support base.

In launching his bid for the presidency, Prabowo followed classic guidelines of textbook populism. Steven Levitsky and James Loxton (2013, 110), for example, developed three characteristics for populists: "First, populists mobilise mass support via anti-establishment appeals, positioning themselves in opposition to the entire elite. Second, populists are outsiders, or individuals who rise to political prominence outside the national party system. Third, populists establish a personalistic linkage to voters." Further, Levitsky and Loxton (2013, 10) distinguished between maverick populists, who are "political insiders who abandon established parties and make personalistic, anti-establishment appeals," and movement populists, who "emerge from social movements and maintain grassroots, rather than personalistic, linkages." Originating from a wealthy family of political aristocrats, Prabowo clearly had to style himself as a maverick populist—and he did. As Prabowo designed his populist image, he also followed other standard descriptions of populism, such as Di Tella's (1965, 47) reminder that populists generally strive to seek "the support of the mass of the urban working class and/or peasantry." Adopting these key elements of populism, Prabowo decided to portray himself as an outsider heroically

> *Prabowo portrayed himself as an outsider heroically trying to save Indonesia from its decaying democracy*

trying to save Indonesia from its decaying democracy, and he wanted to appeal especially to the rural poor and low-income workers in order to gain power.

To further develop his platform, Prabowo looked to Southeast Asia and Latin America for examples of successful populists. Closest to home, he admired Thai populist Thaksin Shinawatra, who won over the poor in 2001 by promising universal access to healthcare and a three-year debt moratorium for farmers (McCargo and Pathmanand 2005). Using public dissatisfaction with the Thai political system and its rich, Bangkok-based elites, Thaksin built a loyal constituency of low-income farmers in the North and Northeast of the country—where, conveniently, the majority of parliamentary seats were contested. No doubt, Prabowo also liked the fact that Thaksin, like him, was an oligarch, but could nevertheless mobilize the poor. In Latin America, Prabowo was fascinated by Hugo Chavez, who, as he did, had a military background. As Prabowo planned to do himself, Chavez won power in Venezuela in 1998 with the support of rural poor and low-income workers,

To shape his populist image, Prabowo studied the script of Thailand's Thaksin Shinawatra

and he maintained his popularity with calculated attacks on the West and its alleged exploitation of developing countries (Hawkins 2003; Levitsky and Loxton 2013). Prabowo also felt affinity to Chavez's radical rhetoric. Pledging to sweep the established parties "from the face of the earth," Chavez promised that Venezuela's "rotten elites" would "soon be consigned to the trashbin of history" (Levitsky and Loxton 2013, 124). As we will see below, Prabowo later borrowed heavily from Chavez's script book.

To be sure, Prabowo did not suddenly come up with the idea of a populist challenge—he had developed it gradually since the mid-2000s. In fact, his ambition to be president dates back even further, as he had been assigned by his father to fulfill the family's political destiny. Born in 1951, Prabowo was part of a powerful clan that traced its ancestry to Javanese aristocrats of the early 1800s (Purdey 2014). His father was Sumitro Djojohadikusumo, an economist, while his grandfather was Margono Djojohadikusumo, the founder of the Indonesian National Bank. Sumitro was a trade and finance minister in several cabinets in the 1950s, but had to flee the country in 1958 because of his affiliation with anti-centralist rebels in Sumatra and Sulawesi. Thus, Prabowo grew up in Singapore, Hong Kong, Kuala Lumpur, Zurich, and London, where he graduated from the American School. Upon the family's return to Indonesia in 1967, Sumitro encouraged Prabowo to enroll in the military, aware that this was the most promising path to political power (Suharto and the armed forces had taken over government in 1966). Prabowo was Sumitro's only male, Muslim offspring (Prabowo's brother Hashim Djojohadikusumo is Christian), and so Sumitro tasked Prabowo with pursuing a military and political career, whereas Hashim was groomed to take over the family's business interests. While Prabowo graduated from the armed forces academy in 1974, it took him one year more than planned: he was penalized for insubordination, offering an early insight into his hot-blooded temperament.

Initially, Sumitro's plan worked even better than expected, as both Prabowo and Hashim turned into quintessential insiders of Suharto's New Order regime. Prabowo rose rapidly through the ranks, clearly helped by his father's status as a member of the Suharto government between 1968 and 1978. More importantly, however, Prabowo married Suharto's daughter Siti Hediati Hariyadi, or Titiek, in 1983. This made Prabowo part of the president's inner circle, and also helped to promote Sumitro's and Hashim's business interests. After leaving the cabinet in 1978, Sumitro founded a consultancy firm and put Hashim in charge of much of its operations. According to *Forbes* magazine, "Hashim's first big deal came in 1988, when he took over a UK-owned cement company. In that deal, as in subsequent ones in the 1990s, he worked his family connections to get the necessary government approvals and access to easy credit. He…enlisted his sister-in-law… as a co-investor in several projects, and his ambitions began to soar."[13] Hashim made no apologies about his status as a rent-seeking regime insider, telling *Forbes* that "I had connections. I've never hidden the fact. I made use of those connections. Why wouldn't I?" Prabowo, meanwhile, continued his ascent to the upper echelons of the armed forces leadership, gaining command of the special forces and the rank of brigadier-general in 1995—the first of his graduating class to be made a general (Lee 2013, 16). Three years later, as Suharto's regime reached its end, he was promoted to three-star general and commander of the strategic reserve.

But the fortunes of Prabowo's clan came crashing down together with Suharto's rule in May 1998. In the period leading to the long-time autocrat's resignation, Prabowo lost an epic power struggle with the then military commander, Wiranto (Mietzner 2009). Sacked from the strategic reserve, Prabowo went to see Suharto's replacement, B.J. Habibie, to demand his reinstatement—a move many interpreted as an attempted coup.[14] Years later, Prabowo stated that he "almost" launched a coup on that day, and that he now "regretted" not actually having done so.[15] Subsequently, Prabowo was discharged from the armed forces for his involvement in the disappearance, torture, and killing of several anti-Suharto activists in late 1997 and early 1998. In public statements, Prabowo admitted to some of these incidents, but denied his responsibility for others, saying that the kidnapped activists were under "preventative detention."[16] Nevertheless, Prabowo was the big loser of the 1998 regime change. Bitter and feeling ostracized by the elite that had previously heaped flattery on him, Prabowo left Indonesia for Jordan, where his friend Crown Prince (and later King) Abdullah offered him protection. Hashim, for his part, moved to London; as was the case with many of his Indonesian tycoon friends, the Asian Financial Crisis had hit his interests hard. Hashim had to negotiate a debt-restructuring deal with the Indonesian government, and was even temporarily arrested during a brief visit to Jakarta in 2002 over lending-limit violations by one of his banks.

Accordingly, like many other would-be populists before him, Prabowo internalized a strong sense of rejection by the ruling elite. His unceremonious dismissal from the armed forces left a deep wound

Prabowo's 1998 dismissal from the armed forces left a deep wound to his pride, feeding his ambition for a comeback

to his pride, feeding his ambition for a comeback and revenge against those who had wronged him. In this, he was similar to Chavez, whose drive for power partly originated with his marginalization from the military in the mid-1980s and his discharge from it after the failed 1992 coup. In Prabowo's case, his indignation was aggravated further by his conviction that it was not only him, but also his family, who had been dishonored. Indeed, he identified his brother's arrest as the moment he decided to run for the presidency: "I thought, 'This is the height of injustice. We are becoming a banana republic.'"[17] But it was this very "banana republic" that offered the brothers opportunities to rise from the ashes. Prabowo, now divorced from Titiek, returned to Indonesia in the early 2000s, building a business empire in the natural resource sector. Using his connections to former military colleagues and old friends in private business, he gained access to bank credits that fueled his business expansion. By 2014, he had a net worth of US$150 million. Similarly, Hashim—having obtained generous debt-restructuring conditions in Indonesia—invested in oil fields in Kazakhstan, which he sold in 2006 for a rumored net profit of around US$600 million.[18] In November 2013, *Forbes* ranked him 42nd on the list of Indonesia's richest persons, with an estimated fortune of US$700 million.

Prabowo's public profile as a populist took shape between 2002 and 2008, when he began to prepare his presidential campaign. In 2004, he entered the race to be the presidential nominee for the Golkar party, Suharto's former electoral machine. However, the candidacy went to his 1998 nemesis, Wiranto, further strengthening Prabowo's belief that the path to the presidency through established political forces was blocked for him. Consequently, he began the process of transforming himself into a maverick populist. In December 2004, he assumed the leadership of the Indonesian Farmers' Harmony Association (Himpunan Kerukunan Tani Indonesia, HKTI). Convinced that, like Chavez and Thaksin, he needed to mobilize the rural poor to get elected, he hoped that the HKTI chair would give him the image of the people's advocate. In the lead-up to the 2009 presidential elections, Prabowo founded his own party, the Great Indonesia Movement (Gerakan Indonesia Raya, Gerindra). By choosing the term *gerakan* (movement), he echoed the chorus of anti-party sentiments in society, and the reference to Indonesia's greatness—which he aimed to restore—gave a taste of Prabowo's ultra-nationalist agenda. Moreover, from around 2007 onward, Prabowo began to wear a Sukarno-style safari outfit, tapping into the nostalgia for Indonesia's founding father. He also increasingly copied Sukarno's oratory style, while pronouncing some words with a Javanese accent similar to that Suharto had used.

While much of Prabowo's appeal to the lower classes and his mimicking of populist-nationalist icons was part of a systematic image campaign, his disdain for the elite and for democracy was genuine.

He had grown obsessively distrustful of politicians, withdrawing to a ranch on the outskirts of Jakarta, where he surrounded himself with loyalists—and animals. Asked why he loved animals, he responded in 2013, "When we grow up and see human nature, there's betrayal, perfidy, lying....But some of these animals are very basic....They are loyal to you."[19] Similarly, he believed that democracy was not suitable for Indonesia as its citizens had not yet graduated from the very "human nature" he so despised. In 2001, he told a journalist that "Indonesia is not ready for democracy....We still have cannibals, there are violent mobs."

While Prabowo's appeal to the lower classes was often manufactured, his disdain for democracy was genuine

Instead, he continued, a "benign authoritarian regime" would be more appropriate.[20] In line with this thinking, he named Lee Kuan Yew and Mahathir Mohammad as his idols—both long-time autocrats (in addition to Thaksin and Chavez, whom he quite obviously admired and copied).[21] And Prabowo had a clear idea of how he wanted to restore Indonesia to its pre-democratic glory: by reviving the 1945 constitution, the document upon which Sukarno and Suharto had built their autocratic regimes. Between 1999 and 2002, this 1945 constitution had been extensively amended, turning Indonesia into a competitive electoral democracy. Resurrecting the original 1945 document would have abolished these democratic innovations, including direct presidential elections and institutional checks and balances.

But Prabowo's self-stylization as a maverick populist made him dependent on the political mood in the electorate. He could only succeed if a majority of voters believed that the existing democratic system was beyond repair. In 2009, this mood clearly didn't exist; Yudhoyono was popular, and voters were inclined to return him to office. Thus, Prabowo's radically populist campaign fell flat (Tomsa 2009). Gerindra only gained 4.4 percent of the votes in the parliamentary elections. This result was not enough to enable Prabowo to run for president. Instead, he had to accept an offer by Megawati to join her ticket as deputy. Unsurprisingly, the pair lost against Yudhoyono in a landslide. But as shown in the previous section, 2014 offered a dramatically different prospect: Yudhoyono was barred from running again, and his lackluster second term served to deepen public dissatisfaction with the status quo. With Yudhoyono out of the way, and only tired, unpopular mainstream politicians left to confront him, Prabowo believed that 2014 was his year. The opinion polls of 2011 and 2012, which Prabowo tended to top, appeared to confirm this view. However, a more detailed look at the polling data told a different story: Prabowo's lead over Megawati, a political has-been, was superficial; and a majority of voters remained satisfied with the democratic system. In brief, while attracted to Prabowo, the Indonesian electorate seemed to wait for an alternative—one that embodied their longing for renewal and more populist leadership, but did not come with authoritarian baggage.

Jokowi's Technocratic Populism

This alternative came in the form of Joko Widodo, or "Jokowi." Much more so than the crude and polarizing populist Prabowo, who thought that most Indonesian citizens agreed with him on the need for comprehensive regime change, Jokowi aggregated the multifaceted and often contradictory viewpoints of the Indonesian electorate in the early 2010s. As discussed, there was significant discontent with Yudhoyono's rule, and certainly the electorate was searching for an antipode to Yudhoyono to replace him: someone who prioritized action over rhetoric; substantive communication over pompous speeches; and genuine interaction with the community over stage-managed ceremonies. Most Indonesians also wanted a fairer distribution of the wealth generated by the natural resource boom of the Yudhoyono period. But polls showed too that there was no mood for a democratic reversal of the kind that Prabowo advocated. A majority of Indonesians were generally satisfied with the state of affairs. In an opinion survey taken in December 2012, 68 percent of Indonesians stated that overall the country was on the right track; 70 percent thought that their economic conditions were better than or the same as a year ago; and only 12 percent believed that, under certain conditions, Indonesia could adopt a nondemocratic system (SMRC 2014c, 41, 53, 15). Apparently, most Indonesians were open to a populist alternative, but it needed to be efficiency-oriented rather than demagogic, inclusive rather than exclusive, and democratic rather than authoritarian. In other words, what the majority of Indonesians longed for was a pragmatic, or technocratic, form of populism-lite.

Jokowi was the almost pitch-perfect personification of this longing for moderate, intra-systemic populism. Born in 1961 in the Central Javanese town of Solo, Jokowi is more than a decade younger than Yudhoyono and Prabowo, removing him from many of the old elite struggles under Sukarno and Suharto. Even more importantly, Jokowi was not born into a bureaucratic, military, or political clan, as most other Indonesian politicians had been. Instead, he was part of a lower middle-class family—his father was a carpenter and his mother a housewife. In his autobiography, Jokowi stressed that he had been born "in the cheapest room" of a local hospital (Endah 2012, 21), clearly trying to prevent the impression that he had enjoyed upper-class privileges. Nevertheless, hospital births were out of reach for most poor Javanese in the 1960s, and it indeed appears that Jokowi's family, while not well-off, was not poor. To be sure, his family had to move several times during his childhood, and was once "evicted" (*digusur*) from one of its rented homes (evictions are a politically salient issue in Indonesia, with many citizens experiencing expulsions from their houses in order to make room for development projects).[22] But Jokowi attended good schools, and after graduation, he entered the prestigious Gadjah Mada University (UGM) in Yogyakarta, where he studied forestry. Jokowi's political opponents have tried during all of his political campaigns to unmask his narrative of humble origins as a clever public relations trick; but while Jokowi may have exaggerated some details of the difficulties he faced as a child, the story of his upbringing is one of rather boring normality—much in contrast to the childhoods of Prabowo or Megawati, for example.

Jokowi's early years were marked by a pronounced lack of interest in politics or ideological debates. While his father was a "very, very low-ranking member of the security guards of the PDI"[23] (the Indonesian Democratic Party, the successor to Sukarno's party founded in the 1920s), there is no indication that Jokowi was attracted to party politics.[24] Similarly, his father had books containing Sukarno speeches in his home, but Jokowi does not appear to have studied them. In his memoirs, Jokowi makes no reference to PDI or Sukarno playing any role in his intellectual development. Instead, he mentions the

> *Jokowi was the personification of this longing for moderate, intra-systemic populism*

Student's Council (Dewan Mahasiswa, DEMA)—which had been banned by Suharto in 1978, but continued to operate on some campuses in a clandestine manner—as a venue where he occasionally participated in political discussions. More important than such discussions, in his view, was rock music, which he credits as having a major influence on him (Endah 2012, 33). Predictably, when the student movement started to become more openly critical of Suharto, and when it eventually began demonstrations against him in 1998, Jokowi was only "an observer" (Endah 2012, 34).

Rather than political and ideological, Jokowi's emerging persona was pragmatic, technocratic, and instinctive. His pragmatism, for one, was visible in his decision to begin a career in business. After his graduation from UGM in 1985, he took a job in a state-owned forestry company in Aceh, but soon returned to Solo to open his own furniture enterprise. During his attempts to gain bank credits and open up new markets for his products, he developed a deep-seated aversion toward red tape and corruption. "If you're in business, you see the real world, its problems, and you get ideas about how to fix them with common sense," said Jokowi later.[25] After a difficult start, Jokowi managed to break into European export markets in the early 1990s, leading to a significant expansion of his business. (One of his French business partners gave him the name "Jokowi" because it helped to distinguish him from other Javanese clients with similar names.) By the early 2000s, Jokowi was moderately wealthy—he could send his children to school in Singapore, for example. But as his wealth grew, he became increasingly interested in trying to improve the lives of ordinary citizens, who he believed were unjustly trapped in bad public services managed by incompetent and corrupt officials. "I never forgot where I came from; when I was young, I identified with the small people (*wong cilik*), I was one of them, and now it is time to do something for them," said Jokowi in a later campaign speech.[26] Tellingly, he referred to his conceptually underdeveloped but emotionally powerful sense of justice as "spiritual democracy" (Endah 2012, 35).

It was this mixture between nonideological pragmatism and emotional empathy with the poor that became Jokowi's trademark in his political campaigns. In 2005, he decided to run for mayor in his hometown of Solo, benefiting from the introduction of direct elections for mayors, district heads, and governors legislated one year earlier (Erb and Sulistiyanto 2009). Nonetheless, Jokowi had to be nominated by a political party to get his name on the ballot. He chose Megawati's PDIP, but only partly because of his father's affiliation with the predecessor of that party or his own ideological tendencies. More significantly, "PDIP was the strongest party in Solo."[27] Jokowi won the elections by a small margin, and immediately began to implement his ideas of better public services for the underprivileged. Not unlike Thaksin, he introduced free healthcare and education scholarship programs for the lower classes. He also used a new approach to street vendors, who had typically been the target of extortion and eviction by predatory city officials. Inviting vendors for lunch, he persuaded them to move to alternative sites (von Luebke 2014). In this, he often invoked his own experience of having been evicted, establishing a personal connection that other bureaucrats found impossible to create. Finally, Jokowi began a routine of so-called *blusukan*, i.e., impromptu visits to public places such as markets, where he asked citizens about their concerns. Other targets of *blusukan* included government offices, where he scolded officials when he found their services lacking. Consequently, his popularity skyrocketed, and in 2010 he won reelection with 92 percent of the votes.

Jokowi's pragmatic and technocratic populism, as it took shape in Solo, stood in sharp contrast to the classic populism of Asian and Latin American strongmen.[28] Whether Chavez in Venezuela, Thaksin in Thailand, Erdogan in Turkey, Tsipras in Greece, or Putin in Russia, traditional populists almost invariably appeal to the masses by identifying and condemning collective enemies. These are often the rich or evil Western powers, and often both at the same time. Thus, inclusion of the poor masses is achieved through the exclusion of the "Other" (Levitsky and Loxton 2013). Prabowo adopted this approach almost one-on-one: he attacked Western nations for looting Indonesia's natural resources, and attacked the country's rich for colluding with them. There was no trace of such polarizing rhetoric in Jokowi's speeches or actions. Indeed, he can be described as a "polite" populist (Mietzner 2014b). While he promoted pro-poor policies, he almost apologetically added that "of course I have no anti-rich sentiments" (Endah 2012, 45). In later campaigns, the most confrontational statement he would make about the "very, very rich" was that "they don't understand you as well as I do."[29] Similarly, although he was a moderate nationalist (politically and economically), he harbored no anti-foreign views. On the contrary, he saw engagement with foreign countries and companies as a welcome opportunity for Indonesia's entrepreneurs. And unlike conventional populists, Jokowi did not propagate the destruction of the *ancien régime*; instead, he proposed technocratic improvements to the democratic status quo. It was not surprising, then, that Jokowi also lacked the rhetorical

> *While Prabowo attacked Western nations, Jokowi harbored no anti-foreign views*

talent of his classic populist counterparts. Often, he just muddled through trivial small talk with the audience rather than offering compelling oratory.

Jokowi's breakthrough at the national stage came with the 2012 gubernatorial elections in Jakarta. There, incumbent governor Fauzi Bowo, a bureaucrat with wide elite networks and a lot of cash, seemed invincible. But in a move that Prabowo came to regret, the then presidential frontrunner raised the idea of Jokowi's nomination for the governorship.[30] For Prabowo, this was a largely strategic move. Rather than aiming at victory, he wanted to claim the maverick credentials that supporting a populist outsider would bestow on him. In order to secure Jokowi's candidacy, however, Prabowo's Gerindra needed additional backing to pass the nomination threshold. Megawati eventually agreed to endorse Jokowi's candidacy, although her husband Taufik Kiemas had already pledged PDIP's support to Fauzi. To everyone's surprise, Jokowi defied unfavorable polls and emerged victorious after two rounds of voting (Gammon 2012). Once elected, Jokowi applied his tested Solo formula to Jakarta: he expanded health and education programs, opening the capital's hospitals to the poor; his *blusukan* became the new mode of government; and he pushed through long-delayed plans for a subway. The national media loved Jokowi's narrative, and he loved them back. Soon, news programs were full of Jokowi stories, catapulting the local government star onto the national scene. And while Jokowi was only sworn in as governor in October 2012, by December he registered in national polls as the new favorite for the presidential race. The battle between the confrontational textbook populist, Prabowo, and the technocratic and inclusivist populist, Jokowi, had begun.

Jokowi's Fight for the Nomination

Jokowi's emergence in opinion surveys as the new presidential front-runner in late 2012 and early 2013 (see Table 1) not only completely changed the dynamics of the race for Yudhoyono's succession, it also presented a critical test case against which key claims of the three dominant schools of thought in Indonesian political studies could be measured. For example, would Indonesia's oligarchic and political elite allow Jokowi to stand in the election, or would it use its extensive power to exclude him from contention? If, on the other hand, he was allowed to compete, did that indicate that Jokowi was not much more than a puppet of the vested interests that, supposedly, controlled Indonesia? Or would Jokowi tilt the balance in the struggle between reformers and conservatives in favor of the former, giving the elite no choice but to accept his rise? And what would Jokowi's entrenchment in the upper echelons of Indonesian politics mean for the operations of the party "cartel"—would it lead to new forms of competition, or would the cartelists succeed in using Jokowi as the nominal figurehead of a freshly configured, collusive alliance? Many of these issues already came to the fore during Jokowi's fight for the nomination, which dragged on for much of 2013 and the first months of 2014.

From the beginning, it was clear that Jokowi would have to make political compromises with some segments of the elite as Indonesia's system does not allow for independent presidential candidacies. For the 2014 elections, nominees for the presidency could only be put forward by parties or coalitions of parties that had gained 20 percent of the seats or 25 percent of the votes in the preceding parliamentary elections. Parties, in turn, had to be registered with the Ministry of Justice and Human Rights almost three years before the legislative poll, and they had to be confirmed as electoral participants by the General Elections Commission (Komisi Pemilihan Umum, KPU) 15 months before the start of the campaign. Hence, Indonesia's system contained significant barriers against populists without an organized

Jokowi had no choice but to make political compromises with the elite to gain the presidential nomination

Table 1. Top Candidate in Presidential Opinion Polling, 2011–2013			
Institute	**Time Period**	**Candidate**	**Percentage**
Soegeng Sarjadi Syndicate (SSS)	October 2011	Prabowo Subianto	28
Indonesian Survey Institute (LSI)	February 2012	Megawati Sukarnoputri	22
Soegeng Sarjadi Syndicate (SSS)	May 2012	Prabowo Subianto	26
Indonesian Survey Cycle (LSI)	June 2012	Megawati Sukarnoputri	18
United Data Center (PDB)	January 2013	Joko Widodo	21
Jakarta Survey Institute (JSI)	February 2013	Joko Widodo	18
Center for Strategic and International Studies (CSIS)	April 2013	Joko Widodo	29
Indonesian Institute of Sciences (LIPI)	May 2013	Joko Widodo	23
Cyrus Network	September 2013	Joko Widodo	44
Indikator Politik Indonesia	October 2013	Joko Widodo	47

Source: Data provided by the various institutes.

power base. Even if Jokowi wanted to form his own party, as Yudhoyono and Prabowo had done before the 2004 and 2009 elections, all the relevant deadlines for party formation had passed by the time the new Jakarta governor topped the polls in late 2012. This meant that Jokowi had to rely on securing the nomination by established parties, and while he was not a highly active party cadre, the most realistic possibility was seeking the candidacy of Megawati's PDIP. But trying to get Megawati's endorsement would force Jokowi to step into a minefield of internal party intrigues, dynastic feelings of entitlement, rejection of outsiders, and personal vanity and idiosyncrasies. Ultimately, he decided to take on the challenge, but this decision had a significant impact on his candidacy and, later on, his presidency.

Within PDIP, the path to the 2014 presidential nomination led via Megawati—and Megawati only. In charge of the party since 1993, Megawati had the most extensive powers of all Indonesian party chairpersons (Mietzner 2012b). At none of the post-Suharto PDIP congresses had she faced a challenger, and delegates had invariably given her a full mandate to determine the composition of the central board, party policies, and presidential nominations. Brought up in the palace as the daughter of Indonesia's founding president, Megawati always had a sense of historical importance, and this only grew after she became vice-president in 1999 and president in 2001. In office, Megawati's aloofness was legendary (Crouch 2003), costing her the election in 2004. She failed to regain the presidency in 2009, which left her deeply wounded. Far from accepting responsibility for her electoral defeats, she blamed them alternatively on the party, manipulations by her opponents, or Yudhoyono's treachery (he had been one of her key ministers and had allegedly promised her that he would not run in 2004).[31] It was clear to everyone inside and outside of the party that Megawati stood no chance in any future presidential election, but few had to courage to tell her that. Surrounding herself with loyalists and family members (most notably, her husband and her daughter Puan Maharani), Megawati rewarded obedience and systematically punished criticism of her feudal-dynastic rule. Hence, convincing Megawati to surrender the 2014 candidacy to Jokowi was a delicate affair, which included the task of persuading her that her time was over, and that none of her offspring (she also has two sons from a previous marriage) was qualified to take her place.

Jokowi's approach to Megawati focused on two main goals: first, to gain her personal trust; and second, to undergo a visible transformation from a nonparty independent into a credible PDIP icon. From early 2013 onwards, Megawati and Jokowi began to spend significant amounts of time together. Both understood the political context of these encounters: Megawati wanted to assess Jokowi's suitability for PDIP's presidential nomination, and Jokowi sought to convince Megawati that he was trustworthy and ready for the presidency. However, these issues were not directly addressed; instead, Megawati invited Jokowi to social functions, talking about food, flowers, and other trivial matters.[32] Only occasionally did she reminisce about her father's politico-ideological persona and her own presidency. Jokowi, for his part, used every opportunity to demonstrate his deference: opening doors for her, moving chairs, and even kissing her hand in public. This strategy worked with Megawati, as she told confidants that she grew increasingly fond of him;[33] but it also damaged Jokowi's image as a tough populist keen to cut through old elite interests. Indeed, Jokowi attracted much ridicule for his submissiveness toward Megawati, which seemed to confirm notions that the entrenched elite remained in control, regardless of who

> *Jokowi attracted much ridicule for his submissiveness toward Megawati*

ran for the presidency. In the same vein, Jokowi began to wear party uniforms more frequently, passionately shouted PDIP's trademark slogan "*Merdeka!*" (Freedom!) at events, and increasingly recited Sukarno in his speeches. PDIP, it appeared, was in the process of acquiring Jokowi, rather than the other way around.

Pointedly, Megawati did not rely solely on personal instincts to vet Jokowi. Rather, she set up a team to provide her with advice. Initially founded in early 2013 to draft PDIP's election strategy, the "team of 11," as it was soon called, consisted mostly of academics from Jakarta, Bandung, Yogyakarta, and Surabaya. Its key figure was Andi Widjajanto, son of former general and PDIP grandee Theo Syafei. Starting from mid-2013, Andi's team changed its focus more and more toward evaluating Jokowi's fitness for office, and his prospects of winning if nominated. The team also tried to assess Jokowi's loyalty to PDIP: for instance, team members searched for (and found) photographs of Jokowi's father wearing a uniform of PDI's security forces.[34] By November, the team told Megawati that she should refrain from seeking the nomination herself, and recommended that she give Jokowi the nod. Megawati seemed to be in agreement, but asked for further input on the matter. It was only in February 2014, two months before the legislative elections in April, that Megawati informed the team that she had decided in favor of Jokowi. However, even Jokowi was not told about this decision, as Megawati and the team continued to discuss the best timing for the announcement of the nomination. "Of course I guessed in January or February that she was leaning towards me; but I was only told a few days before the official announcement,"

Jokowi recalled later.[35] Finally, the party informed the public on March 14 that Jokowi was its nominee.

Unsurprisingly, all three key schools in Indonesian political studies viewed Jokowi's rise and nomination, and the upcoming presidential contest with Prabowo, through their own analytical lenses. For oligarchy theorists, Jokowi had been appropriated by the old elite, which used his popularity to cement its power. Winters, for example, viewed Megawati as a "hidden" oligarch, with Jokowi dependent on her and other oligarchs' support (Winters 2013). Similarly, Vedi Hadiz found that there was no fundamental difference between the two candidates, Prabowo and Jokowi, "because basically the existing election format does not give a lot of opportunities for alternative powers to be involved in the political contestation" (Hadiz 2014). For cartelization scholars, the future of Indonesia's democracy and its party cartel depended on "the choice by Indonesian voters whether to reject Prabowo's rogue gallery, and the choice by Jokowi whether to deliver its decisive defeat not just on election day, but afterwards"—i.e., by building a noncartelistic government (Slater 2014). Pluralists, on the other hand, insisted that—Jokowi's relationship with Megawati notwithstanding—his candidacy constituted a novelty in Indonesian politics, marking the first time a middle-class citizen had a realistic shot at the presidency. Moreover, they interpreted the elections as a major battle between Indonesia's pro-democracy and regressive forces, with Jokowi representing the former (Aspinall 2014a). As in their previous work, pluralists declared the outcome of this contest uncertain, although Jokowi entered the campaign for the parliamentary elections in April 2014 with a 29 percent margin over Prabowo (Mietzner 2014b).

> *All three schools in Indonesian political studies viewed Jokowi's rise through their own analytical lenses*

The Parliamentary Elections: First Cracks Emerge

Prior to his nomination, Jokowi had been the undisputed poster boy of Indonesian politics, a seemingly flawless media darling who held the promise of reform in a society plagued by decades, centuries even, of the machinations of a patronage-cloaked elite. But the parliamentary elections, the campaign for which commenced two days after Jokowi's nomination, changed all of that. His official anointment dragged Jokowi into the lowlands of mundane elite politics, turning him from a polite, above-the-fray populist into a "normal" politician who had to campaign and engage in intra-elite negotiations. This descent into the day-to-day routine of politics left Jokowi severely damaged. Indeed, the start of the parliamentary campaign marked the beginning of an unprecedented decline in his popularity—a collapse that would shrink, and eventually dissolve, his once commanding lead over Prabowo. Four developments in the parliamentary campaign brought Jokowi's weaknesses into the spotlight: first, the campaign exposed Jokowi's lack of a detailed program, or at least his inability to articulate one; second, it made his outwardly subservient relationship with Megawati a central theme of public discussion; third, it highlighted and intensified internal frictions within PDIP; and fourth, it led to a level of organizational chaos in the Jokowi camp that did not bode well for his future political operations.

To begin with, Jokowi's refusal to develop a programmatic platform for the parliamentary campaign strengthened the view of many critics that he was an intellectual and ideological lightweight. Although he was now the officially declared presidential nominee of his party, Jokowi took the view—shared by the PDIP leadership—that he should not address his future government agenda during the campaign. As Andi Widjajanto, who Megawati appointed as head of Jokowi's personal campaign team, explained: "We will reject any questions about his presidential platform; we will just say that we'll talk about that during the presidential campaign—now we just will call on people to vote for PDIP."[36] True to his word, Jokowi's campaign events mixed *blusukan*-style small talk with voters and short speeches, in which he made no reference to any plans he or his party may have for Indonesia's future (Gammon 2014). "Ladies and gentlemen, it is important that PDIP win, and that we win big, so that we have a large majority"[37]—this or similar statements formed the core of his stump speech. Given that his technocratic populism rested on a number of key conceptual and practical convictions (for example, a strategic emphasis on public service improvements, a strong belief in transparency, and a deep-seated resentment of corruption), it is curious that Jokowi and his team decided not to include them in a brief presidential agenda. Arguably,

Jokowi's programmatic silence was a major strategic blunder, and an important factor in the decline of his popularity during and after the parliamentary campaign.

The campaign also led to a public—and very damaging—dissection of his relationship with Megawati. Early in the campaign, Prabowo and his associates coined the term "puppet candidate" (*calon boneka*) to insinuate that Jokowi was simply Megawati's proxy. In a speech on March 28, Prabowo rhetorically asked the crowd: "Do you want to be led by someone…who is a puppet candidate?…A puppet presidential candidate who sings lullabies to the people?"[38] On social media, Prabowo's associates spread a picture of Megawati holding a baby-sized Jokowi close to her chest. The picture became an Internet sensation. It also didn't help that Megawati declared in early April that she had "ordered" Jokowi to become PDIP's presidential nominee, calling him an "official of the party" (*petugas partai*).[39] Jokowi, for his part, did little to defuse widespread suspicions that he was Megawati's marionette. As a result, questions about Jokowi's political independence took deep roots in the electorate. In an opinion survey in June and July 2014, 44 percent of respondents said that they were aware of rumors that Jokowi was "controlled" by Megawati (SMRC 2014b, 18). Of those 44 percent, 53 percent stated that they "strongly believed" or "believed" that the rumors were true. Tellingly, even 38 percent of his supporters believed that Jokowi was steered by Megawati. The puppet candidate issue continued to fester throughout the campaign, and complicated Jokowi's preparations for the later presidential contest.

On social media, Prabowo's campaign spread a picture of Megawati holding a baby-sized Jokowi close to her chest

While the public viewed Jokowi's close ties to Megawati as a political burden, both her family and the party were deeply divided over Jokowi's nomination. Megawati's daughter, Puan Maharani, only learned about Jokowi's candidacy after her mother had already made the decision. It was no secret that Puan had ambitions to run in the elections herself, possibly as running mate to a candidate from another party. After the announcement of Jokowi's nomination, she found it difficult to show any enthusiasm for her mother's choice. In fact, she openly stated her indignation that the position had gone to someone from outside the Sukarno family. In an interview with the newsmagazine *Tempo* in April, Puan claimed that "at the grassroots, they had hoped that the Sukarno family would regain power."[40] Asked whether she viewed Jokowi as an asset or a liability, she could only bring herself to acknowledge that "Jokowi is a cadre. Cadres are assets." Driven by her displeasure, Puan tried to obstruct Jokowi's campaign during the parliamentary elections. As the head of PDIP's overall election team, she refused to approve the production of television advertisements that promoted Jokowi's candidacy. Instead, she sponsored ads that showed herself as the party's protagonist. She only gave in after Jokowi insisted late in the campaign that the party needed to make use of his popularity. But even then she refused to use party funds for the ads, forcing Jokowi's allies to collect money to pay for them. One of Jokowi's associates recalled that "it was a circus. Puan just didn't want to promote Jokowi, only herself. I had to get the money from our friends and bring it directly to the television station, only then did they put the ad on."[41]

But it wasn't only Puan who felt that Jokowi was an annoying intruder. Megawati's daughter had always possessed a very strong sense of entitlement, believing that the leadership of PDIP (and possibly of the country) was her birthright. In an interview in 2014, Puan called it a matter of "ethics" that PDIP had to be led by a member of the Sukarno family.[42] As Puan was the politically most active offspring of Megawati, her statement could only be read as an implicit claim to her mother's succession—and an announcement that she would fight anyone challenging it. Therefore, Puan's opposition to Jokowi was no surprise. However, the skepticism about Jokowi extended even into PDIP's central board. Among its 26 members, Jokowi had only one reliable ally: Maruarar Sirait, the party's deputy chair for youth and sport. Maruarar was the son of an old PDIP grandee, Sabam Sirait, and thus felt a certain degree of independence. All other members had obtained their positions through Megawati's or Puan's patronage, and they feared that Jokowi's rapid ascent to the party's upper echelons could threaten their own positions within PDIP. Although Jokowi was their party's candidate, the majority of central board members had little interest in his victory. A Jokowi presidency, they suspected, would lead to significant power shifts in PDIP, sidelining Megawati's old networks in favor of Jokowi supporters. As a result, PDIP's senior leaders extended little assistance to Jokowi during the parliamentary campaign. Rather, they focused on their own candidacies for legislative positions. Even when Jokowi visited their constituencies, they ensured that their own campaign posters were as prominent as Jokowi's.[43]

To be sure, the lack of support from PDIP was only one of the factors in the organizational chaos that marked the Jokowi campaign. Many of the campaign's defects were self-inflicted. Complementing the programmatic disorientation of the campaign, its technical implementation was equally uninspired. Plans were made and cancelled at short notice, leaving many supporters and local campaign workers disappointed. In some areas, Jokowi's visit was firmly announced, although it had been clear for some time that he would be unable to come. From West Sulawesi to West Java and Nusa Tenggara Timur, crowds assembled only to be told that Jokowi "sent his apologies" for not making it.[44] In some cases, disillusioned masses spontaneously held Jokowi look-alike contests to fill the vacancy. Meanwhile, the "real" candidate made his way through the traffic jams of Java, often in small sedans or buses. Long delays were customary, with an exhausted Jokowi often appearing at midnight for events that had been scheduled to begin five hours earlier. The press corps, usually sympathetic to Jokowi, complained about the unprofessional organization of the campaign, with journalists frequently lost for hours after being cut off from the convoy. Moreover, reporters found very little to write about: the mechanical routine of *blusukan* and program-free speeches made many scratch their heads about what to file to their newsrooms (Mietzner 2014b).

Jokowi's ramshackle campaign was particularly damaging because his rival, Prabowo Subianto, put on a ruthlessly executed show of successful electioneering. Indeed, Prabowo's campaign had everything that Jokowi's did not: a strong message, a united party, and a professional campaign apparatus. In terms of Prabowo's message, it was as crude as it was effective. Presenting classic populist campaign rhetoric, Prabowo claimed that Indonesia's wealth was being looted by foreigners and their cronies; that the political elite stank of corruption; and that only he could save the nation. Prabowo even managed to weave Jokowi into this narrative by not only featuring him as Megawati's puppet, but also as a stooge of foreigners (*antek asing*). Unlike Jokowi,

Prabowo had a unified party, Gerindra, behind him. Finally, Prabowo controlled a formidable campaign machinery. As Jokowi stumbled from one campaign event to the next, Prabowo chose his appearances carefully. He flew in by private plane to one or two events a day before retiring to his private ranch in Hambalang, West Java. And unlike Jokowi, who rejected suggestions of a big event in Jakarta's main stadium, Prabowo was aware of the importance of such demonstrations of power. On March 23, Prabowo arrived at the stadium in a helicopter, drove around in an open van, mounted a horse in a parade of his paramilitary troops, and delivered a rousing speech into a Sukarno-style microphone. As the Western media and liberal Jakartans talked in horror about Prabowo's Mussolini-style parade, Prabowo proudly told a friend that "now Indonesians can choose: do they want a village boy as president, or do they want a real leader?"[45]

> *Prabowo's campaign had everything Jokowi's did not: a strong message, united party, and professional campaign apparatus*

The outcome of the parliamentary elections on April 9, 2014, exposed the first signs of significant cracks in Jokowi's image. While PDIP gained 18.95 percent of the votes and became the strongest party (see Table 2), this was well below the expectations of party leaders and Jokowi himself. Jokowi had regularly stressed that PDIP needed to "win big" in order to get him, as would-be president, a stable majority in parliament. Some pollsters had predicted a result of up to 37 percent, lulling many PDIP functionaries into false hopes for a huge triumph.[46] Amidst the collective disappointment in the party, the word of the "failed Jokowi effect" made the rounds, damaging the candidate's aura of invincibility. Of course, party leaders had willfully ignored warnings by other pollsters that had seen PDIP at or below the 20 percent mark, and which had warned that even Yudhoyono at the height of his power had only managed to lift his Democratic Party (PD) to a maximum level of 21 percent. But more worrying than PDIP's result were other numbers that began to trickle in on voting day. An exit poll showed that 43 percent of voters would have opted for Jokowi and 27 percent for Prabowo (SMRC 2014a, 28). Hence, Jokowi's 29 percent margin had shrunken to 16 percent in the course

Table 2. Parliamentary Elections, April 9, 2014, Results

Party	Percentage	Seats	Post-Election Nomination
Indonesian Democratic Party of Struggle (Partai Demokrasi Indonesia Perjuangan, PDIP)	18.95	109	Joko Widodo
Party of the Functional Groups (Partai Golongan Karya, Golkar)	14.75	91	Prabowo Subianto
Great Indonesia Movement Party (Partai Gerakan Indonesia Raya, Gerindra)	11.81	73	Prabowo Subianto
Democratic Party (Partai Demokrat, PD)	10.19	61	None*
National Mandate Party (Partai Amanat Nasional, PAN)	7.59	49	Prabowo Subianto
National Awakening Party (Partai Kebangkitan Bangsa, PKB)	9.04	47	Joko Widodo
Prosperous Justice Party (Partai Keadilan Sejahtera, PKS)	6.79	40	Prabowo Subianto
United Development Party (Partai Persatuan Pembangunan, PPP)	6.53	39	Prabowo Subianto
Party of National Democrats (Partai Nasional Demokrat, Nasdem)	6.72	35	Joko Widodo
People's Conscience Party (Partai Hati Nurani Rakyat, Hanura)	5.26	16	Joko Widodo

* but supported Prabowo Subianto; Source: Indonesian Election Commission.

of the campaign. Jokowi's pragmatic and technocratic populism-lite, it seemed, was increasingly under threat by Prabowo's powerfully unleashed ultra-populism. Gerindra had doubled its 2009 result to hit 11.8 percent, making it Indonesia's third-largest party. No doubt,

Prabowo was on the rise, setting up a showdown between two very different versions of populism in the upcoming presidential elections.

The Presidential Contest: Technocratic Populism vs. Ultra-Populism

The presidential race between Jokowi and Prabowo marked a historic watershed in Indonesia's process of democratic consolidation (Mietzner 2014c; Aspinall and Mietzner 2014a). No other election since the end of authoritarianism in 1998 had presented voters with such stark alternatives. The choice between Wahid and Megawati in 1999, and between Megawati and Yudhoyono in 2004 and 2009, were about nuances in personality rather than about the fundamental direction of the country. In 2014, by contrast, Prabowo promised to take Indonesia onto a path of neo-authoritarian and ultra-populist experimentation, while Jokowi represented continued democratization and improvements in public services. Thus, the elections concerned nothing less than the future of Indonesia's post-Suharto democracy. At the end, voters opted to reject Prabowo's populist challenge and endorse Jokowi's lighter version of populist renewal—a renewal that could be carried out in the framework of the existing democratic polity. But Jokowi's victory with 53.15 percent of the votes against Prabowo's 46.85 came after a nerve-racking electoral roller coaster in which Prabowo had temporarily closed the gap with his opponent, and in some polls had even overtaken him (see Table 3). At the beginning of the presidential campaign in early June, Jokowi led Prabowo by 47.8 to 41.5 percent (SMRC 2014b, 13), indicating that his advantage had melted away further since the parliamentary exit poll in April. In the middle of the campaign, Jokowi stood at 46.5 to Prabowo's 44.9 percent—a statistical tie. It was only in the final ten days before votes were cast that Jokowi recovered somewhat, retaking the lead and eventually claiming victory.

> *No election since the end of authoritarianism had presented such stark alternatives as Prabowo and Jokowi*

What explains these ups and downs in Jokowi's electoral fortunes? Why and how did he burn a 39 percent margin between December

Table 3. SMRC Polling Results, Presidential Elections, 2013–2014

Time Period	Joko Widodo, %	Prabowo Subianto, %	Margin, %
December 2013	62.0	23.0	39.0
March 2013	56.0	27.0	29.0
April 2014 (Post-Legislative Election)	52.0	36.0	16.0
May 2014	48.0	39.0	9.0
June 2–9, 2014	47.8	41.5	6.3
June 16–19, 2014	46.5	44.9	1.6
June 30–July 3, 2014	47.6	44.9	2.7

Source: SMRC 2014a and 2014b.

2013 and June 2014, and still emerge as the winner? Several reasons caused his popularity to decline further during the presidential campaign, and they were almost identical to the ones that had troubled him during the parliamentary elections. Jokowi still struggled to present a memorable message; he still found it difficult to defuse attacks on his image—this time concerning his credibility as a devout Muslim; the party still did not wholeheartedly support him, with local PDIP branches showing little interest in promoting his presidency; and his campaign apparatus still compared unfavorably to that of Prabowo. But Jokowi ultimately prevailed because of four key factors: first, he had a vast network of volunteers, which came close to what the populism literature describes as a "movement"; second, the election was decided by class sentiments rather than programmatic messages, with the rural poor turning out in masses to vote for Jokowi; third, Jokowi had access to some oligarchic support, which allowed him to counterbalance Prabowo's otherwise overwhelming advantage in this regard; and fourth, the overall mood of the electorate was not in favor of regime change.

As far as the formulation of a clear message was concerned, Jokowi's team knew that it could not afford to replicate the approach of the earlier parliamentary campaign. It was well aware that the electorate demanded, and deserved, statements by the candidates on key policy areas. Yet Jokowi did not find it easy to amalgamate his convictions into a fundamental platform. One of his key advisers recalled that "Jokowi often told us that voters should just look at what he did in Solo and Jakarta to understand what he stands for. But of course it doesn't work like that."[47] As a compromise, it was decided that Jokowi should present samples of health and education benefit cards during campaign events, a method he had already practiced during the gubernatorial elections in Jakarta in 2012 (Hamid 2014, 100). Apart from that, however, Jokowi delegated the formulation of policies to his expert advisers. These advisers developed high-quality policy platforms for him, but Jokowi was often reluctant to study the documents, let alone internalize and articulate them. It was only for the television debates with Prabowo that he saw the necessity to rehearse some of his team's most important policy ideas. Overall, what emerged was a piecemeal compilation of ideas and proposals, but no overarching campaign message. As Jokowi's popularity continued to drop, his team decided it was time to act: it launched the idea of an urgently needed "mental revolution."[48] When this left commentators unimpressed too, Jokowi released a nine-point plan on July 3, 2014— six days before the election. Despite this last-minute effort, Jokowi's inability to develop a powerful campaign platform remained one of his most debilitating weaknesses.

Jokowi also struggled to neutralize the damaging rumors, insinuations, and attacks that Prabowo kept sending his way. While the "puppet candidate" slogan proved more durable than initially thought, Prabowo's team discovered an even more powerful weapon against Jokowi. Tapping into widespread suspicions that Jokowi was a less-than-devout Muslim, Prabowo supporters started to circulate claims in early May that Jokowi was the son

> *Damaging rumors circulated that Jokowi was the son of a Singaporean Christian*

of a Singaporean Christian. At first dismissed as a bad joke, this smear campaign developed a powerful dynamic of its own. "This campaign was the most damaging of all, and our failure to respond to it was the biggest mistake we made in the entire election," Jokowi said later.[49] Feeling the need to deny that he was a Singaporean Christian in almost every campaign speech, Jokowi surrendered the political momentum to his rival. Pictures of Jokowi's pilgrimage to Mecca in 2003 were distributed among devout Muslim voters, and pro-Jokowi Muslim clerics gave sermons in which they tried to disperse the rumors. Ultimately, these efforts succeeded. According to Jokowi, "in the later phase of the campaign, many clerics came to me and said, 'Sir, initially I believed the rumors, but now I know they are lies.'"[50] In Jokowi's view, his bounce in the polls on the final stretch of the campaign was largely due to "the collapse of the smear campaign." Nevertheless, Jokowi's constant attempts to stem the tide of negative attacks gave him little room to define the campaign in an active rather than reactive way.

During the presidential campaign, Jokowi's relationship with PDIP did not improve—it worsened. As in the parliamentary elections, Puan and her associates in the central board either obstructed or ignored Jokowi's campaign. And once again, Puan was reluctant to transfer funds to the candidate and the party's branches, although an alliance of ethnic Chinese tycoons had given PDIP a large amount of money for Jokowi's campaign. It was only after Megawati was presented with dire polling numbers that she ordered the funds to be transferred to local branches, and instructed them to launch an "all-out" campaign.[51] However, even in the final weeks of the campaign, there was no evidence of intensive campaign activity in PDIP's branches. One functionary of PDIP's East Java branch stated in late June that "we're still waiting for money. If we don't have money, there's not much we can do." But there was also no sense of urgency: "Well, I don't like Prabowo, but I think at the end we can all work together."[52] This indifference pointed to a significant change in the relationship between Jokowi and PDIP's local branches. Prior to the parliamentary elections, the branches had been Jokowi's strongest allies in the party. Unlike the central board, they had called for Jokowi's nomination early on, hoping that his popularity would boost the party's showing in the legislative election, and thus deliver more seats to local PDIP bosses.[53] But for them, Jokowi had disappointed these expectations, and no longer deserved much support. Moreover, local PDIP leaders had spent most of their money during their personal campaigns for seats in April (Aspinall 2014b), and had nothing left to invest in Jokowi's presidential bid.

Similarly, the organization of Jokowi's campaign failed to achieve noteworthy improvements since the parliamentary elections. In fact, even sympathetic foreign observers wrote devastating assessments of the chaos crippling the campaign (Tapsell and Gammon 2014). This was, of course, no surprise. Jokowi had surrounded himself with bright young academics and activists to run his campaign, all deeply committed to him. But only very few of them had ever been involved in an electoral campaign, let alone managed one. Thus, while there was a high concentration of scholarly expertise in Jokowi's team, it lacked a hard-nosed and experienced campaign manager. As a consequence, Jokowi moved from one poorly planned event to another, inching forward in painfully slow car convoys through Java, pushing himself to the brink of exhaustion. One of his advisers recalled that "at one event in the morning, Jokowi was so tired he could hardly stand. So I wrote him a little note with pointers for small talk with the audience. He wouldn't have managed anything else."[54] On Prabowo's side, by contrast, a league of professional advisers scheduled and executed his events. They included Rob Allyn, an American consultant who had worked on the infamous George W. Bush primary campaign against John McCain in 2000. Allyn had assisted Prabowo since the mid-2000s, designing advertising campaigns and advising on overall strategy. Allyn took much pride in his work, claiming that he helped Prabowo "to close a gap of 30 points during the last two months of [the campaign]" (Allyn 2014). Needless to say, Jokowi had no such support, and it showed.

Yet despite these continued problems—which explained the loss of his once huge lead over Prabowo—Jokowi came out on top. One of the reasons for this was Jokowi's large network of volunteers (Suaedy 2014). With PDIP doing little to campaign for Jokowi, the volunteers were an effective substitute. Mostly, they consisted of middle-class professionals who were appalled at the prospect of a Prabowo presidency and felt attracted by what they viewed as Jokowi's sincerity, simplicity, and stress on government transparency. Led by former PDIP politicians disappointed by Megawati and previously apolitical, white-collar employees, the

An active network of middle-class volunteers took the place of Jokowi's unsupportive party

volunteer network spread across Indonesia. While there was little coordination between them—and some of the groups even competed for hegemony—the volunteers worked passionately for Jokowi's cause. Unlike Prabowo's army of campaign staff, many volunteers worked for no pay and even spent their own money on campaign activities. Although it would be problematic to categorize Jokowi as a "movement populist" (given that he owed his rise to his technocratic successes rather than the organization of a grassroots network), the volunteers provided a solid societal foundation for the campaign. This support base compensated for the ineffectiveness of PDIP, and allowed Jokowi to portray his candidacy as a departure, however careful and qualified, from conventional party politics. At the very least, the volunteer "movement" offered evidence that Jokowi's inclusivist, pragmatic populism enjoyed an extent of genuine popular support that Prabowo's professional machine lacked.

The second factor in Jokowi's victory was the unexpected importance of class identity in determining voting behavior. Ignored by most analysts of post-Suharto politics, class affiliation was so strong a factor in 2014 that, arguably, it helped push Jokowi over the line. However, the class factor came with a twist: candidates attracted majority support not from the constituencies they *appealed* to, but from those they *belonged* to. Prabowo, for example, whose populist challenge tried to mobilize lower-class, rural voters, instead was supported by the majority of the middle-class, educated, and urban electorate. Jokowi, by contrast, who in Solo and Jakarta had mostly dealt with urban, middle-class issues such as traffic congestion, gained the majority among the rural poor with low levels of education. An exit poll, taken on the day of the presidential election, found that Prabowo trailed Jokowi by 39 percent to 47 percent in the segment of voters with elementary school degrees—but led Jokowi by 46 percent to 34 percent among university graduates (Indikator Politik 2014, 21–22). Similarly, Prabowo was behind Jokowi by 37 percent to 47 percent among voters with incomes below Rp 1 million (US$100), but led him by 45 percent to 39 percent in the higher-income bracket (above Rp 2 million, or US$200). Prabowo also trailed in rural areas, by 38 percent to 47 percent, while leading in cities by 42 percent to 40 percent. Apparently, the rural poor supported Jokowi because he was seen as one of them, while Prabowo attracted upper-class voters who agreed with him that an Indonesian president needed to have the outlook of a world leader—and not, in his words, of a "village boy."

Jokowi had sensed early on that victory or defeat would be determined by the extent to which he could convince rural, low-income voters that he was still an ordinary man with an ordinary lifestyle. The cheap clothes he wore, the reluctance to polish his speeches, his insistence on chitchat with the people instead of holding grand election rallies—all of those choices were designed to win over the lower classes through personal identification rather than programmatic conviction. "My program was: I am simple (*sederhana*), polite (*sopan*), and honest (*jujur*). That's it. As long as people believed me, I was sure I would win," he stated after his victory.[55] In fact, Jokowi had better instincts than his advisers. On the eve of the first television debate with Prabowo, his key lieutenants insisted that he wear a suit to make him look presidential. Jokowi initially refused, but was convinced otherwise.[56] As it turned out, Jokowi was right: later polls showed that the majority of respondents disliked Jokowi in a suit. His popularity therefore dropped after the first debate, despite a convincing performance (Indo Barometer 2014). But throughout the campaign, Jokowi's hold over the core of lower-class voters remained undisputed—his ratings never fell below 47 percent. Conversely, Prabowo's attempt to attract the majority of the rural masses failed because in spite of his pro-poor rhetoric, ordinary Indonesians saw him as part of the wealthy ruling elite. In a desperate attempt to change this perception, Prabowo claimed in a speech on June 22 that he too came from "poor" origins.[57] However, this claim was so obviously untrue that it failed to make an impact.

> *Prabowo attracted upper-class voters worried about electing a 'village boy,' while poor voters consistently preferred Jokowi*

While it was important for Jokowi to uphold the image of a "man of the people," the third factor in his win was his ability to mobilize some oligarchic support. To be sure, Prabowo was well ahead in this area. Obviously, he had his own wealth and that of his brother Hashim at his disposal. But he also enjoyed the support of Golkar Chairman Aburizal Bakrie, a tycoon with wealth of US$2.45 billion;[58] Prabowo's running mate and PAN Chairman Hatta Rajasa, who was allied with oil trader Muhammad Riza Chalid; and Hary Tanoesoedibjo, a tycoon of ethnic Chinese descent, whose net worth was US$1.35 billion. Their money was needed to fuel Prabowo's massive political machine, which dispensed patronage to community leaders, village heads, and religious figures, in the hope that they would call on their followers to vote for him.[59] In contrast, Jokowi's network was mostly volunteer-based, but his campaign nevertheless needed funds to function. Jokowi had access to such funds through an alliance of establishment figures who supported his campaign: for instance, Surya Paloh, worth an estimated US$100 million, whose party Nasdem was the first outside of PDIP to support Jokowi's candidacy; Jokowi's running mate, Jusuf Kalla, the former vice president and Golkar elder who was worth US$47.5 million; and Luhut Panjaitan, a former minister, general, and Jokowi business partner. This oligarchic support allowed Jokowi to challenge Prabowo's financial dominance, but it also tied him to a range of vested interests that would later afflict his presidency.

Finally, Jokowi also prevailed because Indonesia's overall political mood was not in favor of the radical regime change that Prabowo proposed. This had been a long-time problem for Prabowo, as an absolute majority of voters expressed satisfaction with the democratic status quo for much of the post-Suharto period. But the elections aggravated this issue for Prabowo: in July 2014, the month of the election, 69 percent of Indonesians declared that they were satisfied with the way democracy was practiced—up from 53 percent in October 2013, and the highest level since July 2009, the month of the last presidential election (SMRC 2014c, 28). Indonesians, it appears, are most satisfied with democracy during election periods, when they are in the midst of political activism. For a candidate with an anti-democratic agenda such as Prabowo, this public mood in favor of democracy is a major obstacle. Furthermore, Prabowo made a fundamental mistake in the final stretch of the campaign. In the preceding campaign period, he had been careful not to offer specifics about the alternative political system he wanted to put in place. But in a speech on June 28, Prabowo opined

> *Just when Indonesians were most satisfied with democracy, Prabowo reminded them of his dislike for it —a fundamental mistake*

that direct elections were an unwanted Western import to Indonesia, comparing them to a bad habit such as smoking. In their place, he wanted state leaders to be chosen by semi-elected legislative institutions, as was envisaged by the original 1945 constitution (Aspinall and Mietzner 2014b). He called this a "new consensus," a formulation often used by Suharto.[60] When the media picked up on the comment, Prabowo was forced to deny that he wanted to be a "dictator." At a time when Indonesians were most satisfied with democracy, Prabowo had reminded them of his dislike for it.

Jokowi's triumph, then, was a narrow victory of moderate, intra-systemic, and technocratic populism over an ultra-populist, anti-democratic challenger. It was evident that the majority of Indonesians wanted change, and that they wanted a leader who was as dissimilar as possible from the standard politicians they had grown so wary of. But it was equally clear that most Indonesians rejected the notion of a fundamental replacement of the political system. Jokowi's polite, efficiency-oriented populism accommodated this qualified demand for change much better than Prabowo's bellicosity. Certainly, voters were attracted by the populist elements of Jokowi's personality and platform: the simplicity of his lifestyle, the pro-poor rhetoric, the promise of expanded social welfare programs, and the idea of bringing government, and its leaders, closer to the people. However, they also supported those parts of Jokowi's agenda that set him apart from classic textbook populists, and that made his populism a technocratic form of populism-lite: his pragmatic interest in improving government effectiveness, his refusal to condemn the status quo, and his rejection of anti-foreign sentiments. However, Jokowi's victory does not mean that Prabowo's challenge was ineffective. The opposite is the case: almost 47 percent of Indonesians supported his bid, launched by a man with a dark human rights record, a bad temper, and plans to demolish democracy. Moreover, as the next section demonstrates, the elections did not mark the end of Prabowo's career.

The Aftermath: Forming a New Government

The aftermath of the elections delivered, unsurprisingly, evidence for the often-made observation that elections are never the end of political competition, but only its beginning. Indonesia's post-election dynamics highlighted, first, that despite his defeat, Prabowo remained a key player in politics; second, that his anti-democratic agenda had entered the mainstream discourse; third, that Prabowo's domination of parliament presented significant hurdles to Jokowi and his notion of independent, technocratic populism; and fourth, that Jokowi's partners—far from shielding the president from Prabowo and a hostile parliament—demanded constant rewards for their support during the elections. Indeed, their interventions went so far that Jokowi decided to confront them by temporarily seeking Prabowo's assistance. All these developments had a strong impact on how Jokowi's inclusivist, pragmatic populism, which had won him the election, could be translated into concrete policy steps.

During the presidential campaign, much of the discussion among observers had focused on whether Prabowo really pursued an anti-democratic agenda, or whether his ultra-populist rhetoric was just clever electoral strategizing (Aspinall and Mietzner 2014b). In fact, voters seemed to agree with the latter position: in a post-election poll, 70 percent of Prabowo voters expressed satisfaction with democracy, suggesting that they did not believe he would abolish it (SMRC 2014c, 29). But the election's aftermath produced much proof of Prabowo's authoritarian mindset and the path he would have put Indonesia on had he won. First, his associates fabricated quick counts (samples of voting station tallies taken on election day to project the overall result) to claim that he had beaten Jokowi—despite the fact that all other quick counts by credible research institutes had proclaimed Jokowi the winner (Aspinall and Mietzner 2014c). Second, his team tried to intervene in the official vote count on the ground—an effort that only failed because the General Elections Commission (KPU) decided to upload all tabulations online, allowing civil society groups to check the data.[61] Third, Prabowo declared the election illegitimate and vowed to fight until the "last drop of blood" to overturn it. In a video posted online on July 24, Prabowo likened his struggle to the battle of Surabaya in 1945, when pro-independence groups had fought British troops allied with the Dutch.[62] And fourth, he

> *The election's aftermath produced more proof of Prabowo's authoritarian mindset*

encouraged his followers to attack the building of the Constitutional Court on August 21, when its judges rejected his petition for a revote. He later visited some of them in hospital after the police used force to stop the attackers.[63]

However, the most compelling evidence of Prabowo's long-term intentions came with his legislative initiative for the abolition of direct local elections in late August 2014. Implemented in 2005, the direct elections of governors, district heads, and mayors had been a major step forward in Indonesia's democratization process. Most importantly, it was this electoral mechanism that had allowed Jokowi and similar local leaders (such as Surabaya Mayor Tri Rismaharini) to break through the barriers of conventional party politics and claim a direct mandate from the people. In late December 2013, the Yudhoyono government and parliament had agreed that a new local elections law would maintain the direct elections regime. But in the last weeks of the old parliament's tenure, Prabowo proposed the termination of the direct elections and the return to an indirect vote through local legislatures (the system practiced until 2005). He successfully lobbied the parties that had supported his candidacy to back the move, and on September 26, 2014, parliament passed the initiative into law. Yudhoyono's party, PD, which supported direct elections but demanded some revisions to the existing framework, walked out of the deliberations, handing Prabowo's alliance the majority. Yudhoyono, after suffering much abuse on social media for his stance, subsequently issued an emergency regulation that reinstated direct elections. Initially, the pro-Prabowo parties announced that they would vote down this regulation in parliament, but after Yudhoyono threatened to form a long-term alliance with Jokowi,[64] they grudgingly relented and accepted the resurrection of direct polls.

Thus, while Prabowo was denied the presidency, he found other ways of exerting influence. This influence, in turn, was the result of his effective coalition-building efforts, which united parties excluded from Jokowi's presidential bid into a powerful alliance. Most of these parties, and their leaders, had tried to make deals with Jokowi both before and after the elections, but had been told by the candidate (and, later, president-elect) that he could offer no rewards for their support. Disappointed by this, they turned to, and stayed with, Prabowo. For instance, Golkar's Bakrie had already stitched up an alliance with Jokowi in May, but switched to Prabowo because Jokowi refused to make concrete promises of cabinet representation. Similarly, PAN's Hatta Rajasa had offered Jokowi financial support for his campaign if he was appointed his running mate. When Jokowi refused, he made Prabowo the same offer, which was accepted. In addition, Prabowo could also count on the Islamic parties PPP and PKS, which sensed that they would be sidelined under a secular-nationalist PDIP government. Finally, Prabowo enjoyed the support of Yudhoyono's PD as well, at least temporarily. While it was not officially part of the "Red-and-White Coalition" (Koalisi Merah Putih) that had nominated Prabowo, PD campaigned for him. Like Bakrie and Hatta, Yudhoyono was frustrated that Jokowi, or more precisely Megawati, had cold-shouldered him when he had tried to discuss a possible alliance.[65] In short, Prabowo drew his strength from an alliance of parties and leaders that feared politico-economic marginalization under the Jokowi administration.

Together, Prabowo's coalition and PD began their opposition with firm control over the majority of seats in the parliament and, hence, had the power to undermine Jokowi's plan of running a moderately populist and independent government. In October, Prabowo and his allies captured the speakership of both parliament and the People's Consultative Assembly (Majelis Permusyawaratan Rakyat, MPR), which had—theoretically at least—the authority to decide on presidential impeachments. Furthermore, all chairmanships of parliamentary commissions—the key bodies of decision making in the legislature—went to parties affiliated with Prabowo. This left Jokowi's camp without representation at the top leadership level of parliament, and threatened his presidency with the prospect of executive-legislative deadlock.

> *Without top-level representation in parliament, Jokowi's presidency was threatened with executive-legislative deadlock*

While pro-Jokowi factions in both PPP and Golkar managed to weaken both parties from within and give Jokowi some reprieve, parliament emerged as a firm bastion of opposition to Jokowi's infant rule. Even Prabowo's reconciliatory gesture of attending Jokowi's inauguration on October 20 and congratulating him—a move his advisers had told him he needed to do if he wanted to maintain his chances of running again in 2019—did little to change this constellation. Revealingly, Prabowo's brother Hashim told the foreign media that Jokowi had "a price" to pay for his "betrayal" (i.e., accepting Prabowo's assistance in 2012 and then running against him), and that price was legislative obstruction of his government.[66]

But Jokowi's semi-populist project was not only under threat by Prabowo's conservative alliance. His own supporters also put considerable constraints on him. As explained earlier, Jokowi had to go to some lengths to secure Megawati's nod for his nomination. The submissiveness Jokowi showed toward her damaged his image, and also had serious implications for his presidency. Although PDIP had been a difficult partner for him at best, Megawati and her associates now expected rewards from Jokowi. And they were not the only ones: in order to strengthen his campaign and government coalition, Jokowi had recruited the support of the traditionalist Muslim party PKB; Hanura, the party of former military commander Wiranto; Surya Paloh's Nasdem; and the small PKPI (Partai Keadilan dan Persatuan Indonesia, Party of Indonesian Justice and Unity), headed by former Jakarta Governor Sutiyoso. In addition, as hinted above, Jokowi was supported by a number of oligarchs, including his running mate, Jusuf Kalla. Indeed, his coalition partners had imposed Kalla on him—Jokowi reportedly had preferred the head of the Corruption Eradication Commission (KPK), Abraham Samad. Unquestionably, his allies were useful for him in the campaign: PKB mobilized its network of Islamic boarding schools to fight the rumors that Jokowi was a Singaporean Christian; Surya Paloh's Metro TV was the only television station sympathetic to Jokowi, counterbalancing the pro-Prabowo stations owned by Bakrie and Tanoesoedibjo; and the oligarchs provided much-needed funds. But now that the election had been won, it became evident that it wasn't just Prabowo and his brother Hashim who thought that Jokowi had a price to pay; his associates thought so too.

Jokowi's debt to his backers showed in the formation of the cabinet, which was announced on October 26, 2014. Very few of the ministers were his own pick. The lineup included Megawati's daughter Puan, as coordinating minister for human development and culture; Ryamizard Ryacudu, an ultra-conservative general close to Megawati, as minister of defense; Sofyan Djalil, a Kalla protégée, as coordinating minister for the economy; and Tedjo Edhy Purdijatno, a Nasdem politician, as coordinating minister for political, legal, and security

affairs. Jokowi also named another Nasdem member, a retired bureaucrat formerly with the attorney general's office, as new AG (attorney
general). With this, hopes for a breakthrough in law enforcement and
reform appeared to have been dashed. At the same time, Megawati
did not allow Jokowi to appoint Maruarar Sirait, his only supporter
in the PDIP central board, to the cabinet. For Jokowi, who privately
expressed disappointment about the compromises he had to make, the
cabinet formation was an unwelcome clash with reality. Just a month
earlier, he had pronounced that "this is a presidential system, I appoint
the ministers."[67] Now, presiding over a cabinet determined largely by
his allies, Jokowi had to realize that his much-repeated formula, according to which he only accepted the support of parties that demanded no rewards, had always been improbable. In reality, he was the head
of a coalition government that contained a host of vested interests, but
which did not even have a majority in parliament.

The limitations imposed on Jokowi by his own partners were on
full display when he appointed Megawati's former adjutant, Budi Gunawan, as new police chief in January 2015. It was obvious that this
nomination was the result of Megawati's insistence, given that Jokowi
had earlier refused to appoint him to cabinet—one of the very few cases in which he had successfully withstood the pressure exerted by the
PDIP chairwoman. In rejecting Budi during the cabinet formation,
Jokowi could point to the assessment of the KPK, which had informed
him that Budi was suspected of receiving illegal payments worth millions of dollars. But Megawati subsequently forced Jokowi to overlook
these facts and make him police chief—a move that prompted the
KPK to respond by initiating formal legal proceedings against Budi.
Jokowi then canceled Budi's inauguration, enraging Megawati. The
police, in turn, arrested a KPK commissioner on evidently fabricated
charges. Visibly shaken by these events, Jokowi struggled to explain
to the public what had occurred, and what he planned to do to solve
the problem. In one televised interview, he stutteringly read platitudes
from a prepared text, conveying a profound sense of helplessness.
Deeply shocked, social media activists, his former volunteers, and
many of his voters turned against Jokowi, calling on him to cut his ties
to Megawati and Surya Paloh (who had emerged as the second-most
powerful government patron after Megawati, and who had intervened
more than once in executive business). In a poll taken in late January

2015, Jokowi's approval rating plummeted to 42 percent, down from 72 percent in August 2014.[68]

But Jokowi didn't surrender easily either. Indeed, the Budi Gunawan affair forced him to conclude that he needed to start resisting Megawati's attempts to steer him. Facing the prospect of rapidly losing both his popularity and his grassroots support because of Megawati's constant interventions, he decided that it was time for him to set some limits to her influence. He dropped Budi Gunawan's candidacy in February, and submitted an alternative candidate for approval by parliament. In order to shield himself from a possible Megawati backlash, he reached out to Prabowo, who guaranteed him that he would not use the affair as a trigger for impeachment.

> *The Budi Gunawan affair convinced him he should resist Megawati's attempts to steer him*

By negotiating directly with the opposition, Jokowi demonstrated to Megawati that he had other options, and that he would no longer automatically implement her "suggestions." Thus, while at the beginning of the Budi Gunawan case it appeared as if Jokowi was in an unstoppable spiral of decline, and that his concept of technocratic populism was dead, it ultimately led Jokowi to put a bigger distance between himself and the coalition partners who believed that he was obliged to cater to their wishes.

Even before the relationship with his partners soured in early 2015, Jokowi had demonstrated his willingness to forcefully confront obstacles to his presidential agenda. Most significantly, Jokowi regularly resorted to presidential decrees to implement decisions for which Yudhoyono would have sought parliamentary approval. For example, he launched his landmark program of increased health and education benefits within weeks of coming to office. Ignoring protests by parliament that he needed its authorization, he issued health, education, and welfare cards to millions of Indonesians, expanding the coverage of a previous program started in early 2014.[69] In order to mobilize funds for this hugely expensive project, Jokowi cut fuel subsidies in November, followed by the complete abolition of subsidies for premium gasoline in January 2015.[70] Once again, he did this without consulting parliament (or many of his ministers, for that matter). Moreover, he fired the entire board of the state oil company Pertamina, which had been a hotbed of corruption for decades. And while he listened to external advice in naming the reformist but hesitant Sudirman Said as minister for energy and minerals, Jokowi appointed the much more outspoken economist Fasisal Basri to head a team tasked with restructuring Indonesia's oil and gas sector and, in particular, eradicating the "mafia" that feeds off it. Jokowi, therefore, constrained as he is by the Prabowo-dominated parliament and his own coalition "partners," has shown clear signs that he is prepared to fight for the core components of his platform—namely, the improvement of public services—while finding savings to fund them.

Jokowi's first months in office have also highlighted the character of his very specific form of technocratic populism. Like many Latin American or Asian populists before him, Jokowi sees expanded welfare benefits as the primary criterion of successful governance—and the key to reelection. Hence, his quick launch of new health and education programs was in line with what could be expected of a populist newcomer. Similarly, Jokowi has maintained the man-of-the-people image while president, even flying economy class on several occasions. But Jokowi also did something most other populists would shy away from: cutting fuel subsidies. Indeed, fuel subsidies have been the main dish on many populist menus, from Venezuela to Thailand. That Jokowi, in contrast, was determined to begin his presidency with a cut in subsidies showcases the technocratic element of his populist agenda. To be sure, the January 2015 assimilation of premium gas prices to international market levels allowed him to actually reduce prices, given the rapidly falling global oil price at that time. But Jokowi's aversion to fuel subsidies was principled in nature: "Fuel subsidies are nonsense—they benefit the middle class, the people with cars. We need to free up the money wasted on these subsidies to fund programs that really benefit the poor," Jokowi insisted.[71] Indonesians, then, had indeed elected a populist—but one with a strong fixation on public services management, and one who had to deal with an establishment-led parliament and government coalition that are certain to watch his every move.

Jokowi's Technocratic Populism: Comparative and Indonesian Perspectives

The 2014 presidential elections in Indonesia have presented a rich laboratory for political scientists interested in populism theory and, more concretely, the state of post-Suharto democracy. To begin with, the Indonesian case has challenged one of the most conventional wisdoms of populism literature: that populist challenges are most likely to emerge, and draw much support, in countries stuck in political and/ or economic crises (Pappas 2014; Pappas and Kriesi 2015). In Venezuela, for example, per capita income had halved in the seven years before Chavez's 1998 take-over, and electoral turnout had dropped to 52 percent. All of this pointed to a polity in decay, offering fertile ground for a populist who harshly denounced the status quo. But Indonesia was *not* a polity in severe crisis when Prabowo launched his 2014 bid. Per capita income had tripled between 2004 and 2013 (from US$1,161 to US$3,557), and electoral turnout, while lower than at the beginning of the democratic transition, was above 70 percent. As discussed, support for democracy, and the way it was implemented in Indonesia, was high as well. Consequently, a serious economic or political crisis is *not* a *conditio sine qua non* for a populist challenge; rather, a sense of stasis, or sociopolitical calcification, can be sufficient to drive a population into the arms of a radical populist. This is particularly the case if there is a widespread perception, true or otherwise, that the rich profit more from economic growth than the ordinary population, and that—as Slater pointed out—a small ruling class monopolizes power. Politico-economic stability *per se*, then, is no safeguard against the rise of populists if a significant segment of society feels disadvantaged by, or simply bored with, this stability.

> *Indonesia's 2014 elections presented a rich laboratory for political scientists interested in populism theory and post-Suharto democracy*

Nevertheless, the Indonesian case also shows that overall stable political and economic conditions make it more difficult for a radical populist challenge to *succeed*. While Prabowo gained the support of almost 47 percent of the population, he ultimately failed to convince the majority that the existing polity was irreparable. In his stead, voters opted for a populist with a more moderate outlook, and who lacked many of the characteristics that theorists usually ascribe to populists. In a way, Jokowi was the compromise candidate Indonesian voters sought. Had he not existed, a similar character would have had to be created in order to aggregate and represent the views of the electorate at large. Jokowi's technocratic populism, then, was the result of a significant, but not life-threatening, crisis of confidence into the way Indonesia's democratic leaders—most of all, Yudhoyono—had managed politics in the preceding decade. Jokowi held the promise of change without causing major political upheaval or social disruption, and with that, he perfectly captured the political preferences of the majority. Jokowi's rise also fits into the patterns some theorists identified in recent studies of populism in post-crisis Europe. Takis Pappas and Hanspeter Kriesi (2015), for example, argued that the extent of populist responses in Europe was often directly related to the level of severity of the crisis. Greece, for example, which was worst hit, has seen the most pronounced surge in support for populist parties. But in countries in which the crisis was less serious, the populist surge was limited as well. Using this explanatory model, Jokowi's moderate populism was the product of a moderate crisis.

> *Jokowi's moderate populism was the product of a moderate crisis*

Would it be appropriate, then, to describe Jokowi as a "post-populist," i.e., as a politician who combines elements of classic populism with ideas of neoliberal reforms (Roberts 2000)? Is he comparable to Argentina's Carlos Menem or Peru's Alberto Fujimori, who both were seen as populists, but who stayed away from economic populism once elected? Clearly, there are similarities between Jokowi and these Latin American "post-populists," such as their political pragmatism. But Jokowi has been too strongly supportive of economic nationalism and protectionism to be categorized as a post-populist. Inevitably, as a businessman, Jokowi endorsed the principle of free market competition. However, the general mood in Indonesia has been exceedingly hostile to neoliberalism, especially since the early 2010s. Responding to this, Yudhoyono allowed his Trade Minister Gita Wirjawan (appointed in 2011) to introduce a number of protectionist measures that angered foreign investors. In the campaign, Prabowo tried to top this approach by promising to end what he viewed as the foreign dominance of the Indonesian economy. Jokowi, for his part, chose a more moderate but still determined tone: while rejecting Prabowo's call for a unilateral cancelation of mining contracts with foreign enterprises, Jokowi promised to review them after expiration. After his inauguration, Jokowi shocked some foreign dignitaries at international summits by insisting that Indonesia would only accept foreign investments that benefited the country and population.[72] Therefore, Jokowi's classification as a "post-populist" would be ill-fitted, given the importance of economic nationalism in Jokowi's political profile and society at large.

It is more fruitful to locate Jokowi within a new political paradigm of post-Thaksin Asian populism. The difference between this new form of populism and more classic manifestations of populist appeals is primarily of a political, rather than economic, nature. Jokowi adopted many key aspects of conventional populist concepts: the emphasis on social welfare programs; the cultivation of an image of simplicity and egalitarianism; and the adoption of economic nationalism, albeit reluctantly. But unlike most other populists, whether in Latin America or Asia, Jokowi presented no "Other" against which he could agitate or define his platform. For Thaksin, the campaign against the "Other" (in his case, the rich, the military, and the cronies of the monarchy) was a crucial element of his populist campaign. Importantly, this focus on adversaries continued through his tenure in office, and contributed to his downfall. In this sense, Jokowi learned from Thaksin's failure, or from that of other populists who used belligerent rhetoric to ascend to power, but subsequently found themselves overthrown by the enemies they had created. Jokowi's inclusivist, nonadversarial, and pro–status quo model is what truly sets him apart from other populists. Even India's Modi, who in many other ways is also part of the post-Thaksin generation of populists, could not come to power without an exclusivist appeal to the Hindu majority, and an implicit definition of Muslims as the "Other." Hence, Jokowi's technocratic and inclusivist populism goes beyond Thaksin's interpretation of populism as strategically induced class warfare, but also beyond Modi's religious and cultural chauvinism.

Against this background, what does Jokowi's presidency mean for the study of Indonesian politics? Does the rise of a carpenter to Indonesia's top executive position disprove the claim of oligarchy theorists that the massively wealthy control almost all aspects of political life in Indonesia? Or, conversely, does Jokowi's inability to appoint his own cabinet, and his being forced to hand out rewards to his sponsors, provide evidence for precisely this claim?

Obviously, many of the events *after* the election could be read as a confirmation of the position advanced by oligarchy theorists. To begin with, oligarchs represented in or supporting the Prabowo coalition limited Jokowi's powers by assembling a formidable force in parliament. And their pressure paid off, both politically and materially: Aburizal Bakrie, for instance, was able to secure a US$62 million loan from the government in December 2014 in order to pay compensation to victims of a mud spill triggered by one of his companies in 2006.[73] In exchange, Bakrie softened his opposition to Jokowi somewhat. Parliament also possesses an effective veto power against legislative initiatives launched by the executive, convincing the Jokowi administration to hold back on controversial bills. Moreover, the oligarchs in Jokowi's own coalitions have repeatedly tried to steer him and his administration. Surya Paloh, for instance, had many of his ministerial nominees approved, and he brokered a dubious oil deal with Angola in the first weeks of the Jokowi government.[74] He was also one of the main defenders of Budi Gunawan, using his television station to run a campaign against the KPK. And while Megawati herself is not an oligarch (even not a "hidden oligarch," as claimed by Winters), she intervened regularly in government affairs in order to defend the interests of the established elite. Jokowi, for his part, seemed initially willing to fulfill all demands made by his sponsors, until the Budi Gunawan affair convinced Jokowi that he had to begin emancipating himself.

Despite the intuitive power of the oligarchy theorists' interpretation of Jokowi's rise and election, it is worth recalling that Jokowi was *not* the oligarchs' choice. Rather, Jokowi's emergence as a populist outsider confronted the oligarchs with an unforeseen situation, forcing them to either oppose him by supporting a different candidate or to join him in his campaign. Accordingly, Jokowi was not a puppet of the wealthy and powerful, neither during the election nor afterwards; he was, for them, an unwelcome phenomenon they had to come to terms with. Following Jokowi's election, the oligarchs tried to obstruct,

Does the rise of a carpenter to Indonesia's top executive position disprove the claim of oligarchy theorists?

extort, blackmail, or control him, and some of these attempts worked—and, most likely, will continue to work. But he is still not one of theirs. His nonelite background has kept Jokowi out of the oligarchic club indefinitely. The members of this club will always view Jokowi as a social climber, a foreign object in a closed, exclusive circle. Thus, his election *was* evidence that Indonesia's oligarchs are not omnipotent. It is also important to note that while the oligarchic elite may have influence on him, he also holds power over them. As president, he holds the key to executive decision making, resource distribution, and law enforcement, and his early steps to revamp the oil and gas sector demonstrated his readiness to use this authority whenever he deems it necessary to protect his core agenda. It would be wrong, therefore, to view the power balance between Jokowi and the oligarchs as hopelessly tilted toward the latter. This power balance is more accurately described as intrinsically oscillating.

Another questionable assertion of oligarchy theorists is that the elections, in essence, didn't matter because "alternative powers [were not] involved in the political contestation" (Hadiz 2014). For all the oligarchic intrusions into Jokowi's presidential autonomy, Indonesia would have looked very different under a Prabowo presidency. Aspinall (2015) described Prabowo's agenda as "oligarchic populism"—an agenda that was as inherently anti-democratic as it was focused on protecting his own oligarchic interests. While it is probable that Prabowo would have "tamed" other oligarchs with the same authoritarian methods that Suharto applied during his rule (Winters 2011), he surely would have placed himself at the apex of an oligarchic pyramid consisting of his family, loyalists, and business partners. In the meantime, he would have worked, as announced, toward a recentralized political system along the lines of the Sukarno and Suharto regimes. Jokowi's technocratic and nonconfrontational populism, by contrast, sought to maintain and improve the democratic status quo, with all its opportunities for oligarchs and other societal actors to defend their interests in open competition. The inclusiveness of Jokowi's populism implied that he did not want to declare war on the oligarchic class; while this attitude made him vulnerable to oligarchic interventions, it also led him to defend the existing democratic system against Prabowo's attempt to dismantle it.

Oligarchy theorists are correct, however, in emphasizing that the institutional settings of Indonesian democracy make it hard for nonestablishment figures to compete. Indeed, this was the main factor that forced Jokowi to build alliances with Megawati and other elite actors in the first place. Between 1999 and the early 2010s, the Indonesian elite developed, and routinely tightened, rules that were designed to retain its overall control of the political system. For instance, the very high presidential nomination thresholds for the 2009 and 2014 elections—20 percent of the seats or 25 percent of the votes—effectively ruled out candidacies by nonparty populists. At the same time, the Indonesian elite made it exceedingly difficult to establish new political parties, limiting the opportunities for movement populists to enter the electoral arena. For the 2014 elections, parties needed to have representation in all Indonesian provinces in order to qualify for electoral participation. Similarly, parties wishing to stand in the 2014 polls had to register by August 2011—almost three years before voting day. At that time, Jokowi was still mayor of Solo, and the idea of him running in 2014 was outlandish. Accordingly, when Jokowi emerged as the presidential front-runner in early 2013, he had no party of his own, and had to make arrangements with the establishment if he wanted to stand in the elections. The fallout from the Budi Gunawan case showed, however, that he never really fused with the party that nominated him; on the contrary, it demonstrated that he remained a PDIP outsider.

Jokowi's formation of a cabinet that included fewer parties than were needed to control a majority in parliament also makes it difficult to interpret his presidency through the lens of cartel party theory. Jokowi discontinued both Megawati's and Yudhoyono's practice of building oversized coalitions, which are the main analytical interest of cartel scholars. Moreover, Jokowi experienced increasingly tense relations even with his own party, with some PDIP officials calling for his impeachment as early as January 2015. Subsequently, Jokowi moved toward a more fluid pattern of seeking support from parties on a case-by-case basis, while maintaining a core of permanent partners to fend off threats of impeachment. This state of affairs is hardly consistent with cartelism; instead, it supports the notion proposed by advocates of a pluralist interpretation of Indonesian power relations—namely, that the political arena of the post-Suharto polity remains heavily contested by a variety of forces. This arena contains, among others, oligarchs, traditional party leaders, civil society groups, and populists such as Jokowi, and it would be reductionist to claim that any one of these actors has established dominance over the others. Hence, it is just as problematic to celebrate Jokowi's victory as a sign that pro-reform advocates are now in control than it is to interpret the oligarchic intervention of his government as evidence that the oligarchs have prevailed. Instead, the battle over political hegemony in Indonesia's post-authoritarian regime continues.

For policymakers, and especially international partner governments, this means that Indonesia's democratization process continues to be vulnerable and, indeed, reversible. While a return to authoritarianism had been a taboo topic for mainstream politicians between 1998 and 2014, the 2014 elections and their aftermath have introduced this issue as a politically acceptable discourse. Following the elections, in which he had not even been allowed to stand as a candidate, Bakrie openly spoke about his wish to return to "Pancasila Democracy"—Suharto's term for his authoritarian regime.[75] Consequently, international leaders should refrain from

Praise for Indonesia's democratic progress is well deserved, but often exaggerated

excessively enthusiastic rhetoric about Indonesia being a model Muslim democracy. In recent years, it has almost been obligatory for international visitors to Jakarta to praise Indonesia's exceptional democratic progress.[76] Some of this praise has been well deserved, but exaggerated acclaim is likely to do more harm than good. There is no room for complacency; therefore, Indonesia's partners should treat the country as a young, volatile democracy struggling with a host of political and social problems, and not as a consolidated democracy that needs no further assistance. Concretely, foreign donors that have begun to close down their democracy assistance programs should reconsider their approach (Aspinall 2010). Jokowi's victory, and the thus far successful defence of the democratic project, was in no small part the work of civil society groups, community leaders, and activists—the main beneficiaries of one and a half decades of international democracy assistance. They will need all the help they can get to fend off further challenges to Indonesia's democratic polity.

Endnotes

1. "Jokowi Widodo—Indonesia's Narendra Modi?" *Niti Central,* July 30, 2014.

2. Interview with Susilo Bambang Yudhoyono, Cibubur, December 2, 2014.

3. See for instance, "Nama Ibas Muncul di Kasus Korupsi SKK Migas," *Tribun News,* February 17, 2014.

4. Yudhoyono admitted that he diluted the initial proposal because "there was just too much opposition," and "my ministers were divided" over the issue. Interview with Susilo Bambang Yudhoyono, Cibubur, December 2, 2014.

5. "Kritik SBY Dapat Lemahkan KPK," *Viva News,* June 25, 2009.

6. Interview with Susilo Bambang Yudhoyono, Cibubur, December 2, 2014.

7. "World's Biggest Millionaire Boom? It's in Indonesia," *MNN Post,* September 28, 2012.

8. "Income, a Perilously Widening Gap," *Jakarta Post,* June 5, 2012.

9. "Poverty in Indonesia: Muted Music," *The Economist,* May 3, 2014.

10. Interview with Susilo Bambang Yudhoyono, Cibubur, December 2, 2014.

11. Yudhoyono explained the late improvement of his popularity with his "entry into Twitter land," as he put it, in April 2013. Interview with Susilo Bambang Yudhoyono, Cibubur, December 2, 2014.

12. "Survei: Prabowo dan Mahfud Teratas Jadi Capres 2014," *Kompas,* October 26, 2011.

13. Simon Montlake, "Homecoming," *Forbes,* January 15, 2010.

14. Jose Manuel Tesoro, "The Scapegoat?" *Asiaweek*, March 3, 2000.

15. "Prabowo Menyesal tidak jadi Kudeta Habibie," *Merdeka*, March 2, 2014.

16. "Indonesia's Dark-horse Candidate," *Asia Times*, March 31, 2009.

17. "Lunch with the FT: Prabowo Subianto," *Financial Times*, June 28, 2013.

18. Simon Montlake, "Homecoming," *Forbes*, January 15, 2010.

19. "Lunch with the FT: Prabowo Subianto," *Financial Times*, June 28, 2013.

20. "US Journo's 2001 'Off the Record' Prabowo Interview Details Indonesia 'Not Ready for Democracy,'" *Jakarta Globe*, June 26, 2014.

21. "Lunch with the FT: Prabowo Subianto, "*Financial Times*, June 28, 2013.

22. Jokowi's mother, for her part, couldn't recall the eviction when asked about it by a journalist. She also denied that the family lived in successive run-down houses at the river. "The house was indeed a few hundred meters from a river, but it is located on a street and it is our own house," she said. See "Man of the House, Man of the Moment," *Jakarta Post*, November 20, 2013.

23. Interview with Joko Widodo, Jakarta, September 15, 2014.

24. The PDI morphed into the PDIP in 1999.

25. Interview with Joko Widodo, Bandar Lampung, March 21, 2014.

26. Joko Widodo, campaign speech, Bogor, June 7, 2014, notes by the author.

27. Interview with Joko Widodo, Jakarta, September 15, 2014.

28. The concept of "technocratic populism" has recently been used to describe Ecuador's President Rafael Correa (Torre 2013). However, Correa's leftist, confrontational rhetoric (he was a close ally of Hugo Chavez) made him an ideologue rather than a technocrat primarily focused on government efficiency. Arguably, then, the label "technocratic populism" fits Jokowi better than Correa.

29. Joko Widodo, campaign speech, Bogor, June 7, 2014, notes by the author.

30. It was Hashim who recommended Jokowi to Prabowo. Hashim had met Jokowi in 2008 and had been impressed by his performance as mayor in Solo.

31. Yudhoyono denied ever having given her such a promise. Interview with Susilo Bambang Yudhoyono, Cibubur, December 2, 2014.

32. Interview with a Jokowi adviser, Jakarta, November 18, 2013.

33. Interview with a Megawati adviser, Jakarta, September 26, 2013.

34. Interview with a member of the "team of 11," Jakarta, September 11, 2014.

35. Interview with Joko Widodo, Jakarta, September 15, 2014.

36. Interview with Andi Widjajanto, Jakarta, March 16, 2014.

37. Joko Widodo, campaign speech, Lampung, March 22, notes by the author.

38. "Kampanye di Gunung Kidul, Prabowo Sindir Lagi Capres Menca-mencle," *Viva News*, March 29, 2014.

39. "Megawati: Jokowi Petugas Partai yang Saya Perintah Jadi Capres," *Kompas*, April 5, 2014.

40. "Tak Ada yang Bisa Mengempaskan Saya," *Majalah Tempo*, April 14, 2014.

41. Interview with a senior PDIP politician, Jakarta, April 6, 2014.

42. "Puan Maharani: AD/ART tak Haruskan Trah Sukarno Pimpin PDIP," *Republika*, September 24, 2014.

43. For instance, the first campaign event Jokowi attended in the parliamentary campaign was one organized by Effendi Simbolon, a senior member of the PDIP central board, a vocal Jokowi critic, and a legislative candidate in Jakarta. His campaign posters dominated the event. Personal observations by the author, March 16, 2014.

44. "Jokowi Tak Datang, Massa PDI-P di Polewali Mandar Kecewa," *Kompas*, April 4, 2014.

45. Confidential interview, Jakarta, March 25, 2014.

46. "Indonesia Opposition to Top Legislative Polls: Survey," *Jakarta Post*, April 4, 2014. However, some of these polls had asked respondents whether they would vote for PDIP if Jokowi were its presidential candidate, creating a counterfactual voting scenario. Jokowi's name was not on the ballot.

47. Interview, Jakarta, September 9, 2014.

48. "Misi Revolusi Mental Jokowi," *Kompas*, April 26, 2014.

49. Interview with Joko Widodo, Jakarta, September 15, 2014.

50. Interview with Joko Widodo, Jakarta, September 15, 2014.

51. Interview with a member of Jokowi's campaign team, Jakarta, June 25, 2014.

52. Interview, Surabaya, June 26, 2014.

53. Interview with branch heads at the PDIP national working meeting in Jakarta, September 6, 2013.

54. Interview, Jakarta, September 9, 2014.

55. Interview with Joko Widodo, Jakarta, September 15, 2015.

56. Interview with a member of Jokowi's campaign team, Jakarta, June 9, 2014.

57. Campaign speech by Prabowo Subianto, Jakarta, June 22, 2014, notes by the author.

58. The wealth figures of Indonesian tycoons cited in this study are primarily from *Forbes*'s most recent wealth rankings and the reports of candidates to the KPU.

59. Interviews with pro-Prabowo activists, Madiun, June 28–29, 2014.

60. "Prabowo Sebut Indonesia Produk Barat yang Susah Diperbaiki", *Kompas*, 29 June 2014.

61. "Kembali Ditemukan Dugaan Manipulasi Suara Prabowo-Hatta di Sikka, NTT," *Berita Satu News*, July 16, 2014.

62. The video "Pesan Video Prabowo Subianto, 25 Juli 2014" can be viewed at https://www.youtube.com/watch?v=S9pfcbCzprU.

63. "Pendukung Prabowo di MK Diciduk Polisi," *Tempo*, August 21, 2014.

64. Interview with Susilo Bambang Yudhoyono, Cibubur, December 2, 2014.

65. Interview with Susilo Bambang Yudhoyono, Cibubur, December 2, 2014.

66. "Hashim Tells of Plans to 'Obstruct' Jokowi Govt," *Jakarta Globe*, October 8, 2014; "Subianto's Brother Promises 'Active' Opposition to Jokowi," *Wall Street Journal*, October 7, 2014.

67. Interview with Joko Widodo, Jakarta, September 15, 2014.

68. "Jokowi's Approval Rating Below 50 Percent," *Jakarta Post*, January 30, 2015.

69. The new program included health coverage for 432,000 homeless and otherwise severely disadvantaged citizens in 2014, with this number scheduled to go up to 1.7 million in 2015. See "6,4 Trilyun digelontorkan Kabinet Jokowi untuk KIS, KIP, dan KKS Tahap Pertama," *Detik.com*, October 31, 2014.

70. "Harga BBM Naik, Negara Hemat Subsidi Rp 120 Triliun," *Tempo*, November 18, 2014.

71. Interview with Joko Widodo, Jakarta, September 15, 2014.

72. "Jokowi Tegas, Kepala Negara APEC Termasuk Obama Kaget," *Tujuh News*, November 12, 2014.

73. "Kalla Claims Controversial Lapindo Bailout a Win-Win Solution," *Jakarta Post*, December 20, 2014.

74. "Cari Fee dari Sonangol, Surya Paloh: Sontoloyo Itu," *Tempo*, November 24, 2014.

75. "Ical: Pilkada Langsung Menghilangkah Ruh Pancasila," *Merdeka*, September 11, 2014.

76. "Obama Tells Widodo: Indonesia Is a 'Model' for Majority Muslim Nations," *Wall Street Journal*, November 10, 2014.

Bibliography

Allyn, Rob. 2014. "Every Vote Must Be Counted, Every Voice Must Be Heard," *New Mandala*, July 16. http://asiapacific.anu.edu.au/newmandala/.

Ambardi, Kuskridho. 2008. "The Making of the Indonesian Multiparty System: A Cartelized Party System and Its Origin." PhD dissertation, Department of Political Science, Ohio State University.

———. 2009. *Mengungkap Politik Kartel: Studi tentang Sistem Kepartaian di Indonesia Era Reformasi.* Jakarta: Kepustakaan Populer Gramedia.

Aspinall, Edward. 2009. *Islam and Nation: Separatist Rebellion in Aceh, Indonesia.* Stanford: Stanford University Press.

———. 2010. "The Irony of Success," *Journal of Democracy* 21 (2): 20–34.

———. 2014a. "Indonesia on the Knife's Edge," *Inside Story*, June 17.

———. 2014b. "Indonesia's 2014 Elections: Parliament and Patronage." *Journal of Democracy* 25 (4): 96–110.

———. 2014c. "Popular Agency and Interests in Indonesia's Democratic Transition and Consolidation." In Ford, Michele, and Thomas P. Pepinsky, eds. 2014. *Beyond Oligarchy: Wealth, Power and Contemporary Indonesian Politics.* Ithaca: Cornell Southeast Asia Program Publications.

———. 2015. "Oligarchic Populism and Economic Nationalism: Prabowo Subianto's Challenge to Indonesian Democracy," *Indonesia* (forthcoming).

Aspinall, Edward, and Marcus Mietzner. 2014a. "Indonesian Politics in 2014: Democracy's Close Call." *Bulletin of Indonesian Economic Studies* 50 (3): 347–369.

———. 2014b. "Prabowo Subianto: Vote for Me, But Just This Once," *New Mandala*, June 30. http://asiapacific.anu.edu.au/newmandala/.

———. 2014c. "Prabowo's Game Plan," *New Mandala*, July 10. http://asiapacific .anu.edu.au/newmandala/.

BPS–Badan Pusat Statistik. 2014. *Laporan Bulanan Data Sosial Ekonomi. Edisi 55*. Jakarta: BPS.

Butt, Simon. 2006. "Indonesia's Constitutional Court: A Reform Over-achiever?" *Inside Indonesia*, 87, July–September.

Crouch, Harold. 2003. "Political Update 2002: Megawati's Holding Operation." In Aspinall, Edward, and Greg Fealy, eds. 2003. *Local Power and Politics in Indonesia: Decentralisation and Democratisation*. Singapore: ISEAS.

Di Tella, T.S. 1965. "Populism and Reform in Latin America." In Veliz, Claudio, ed. 1965. *Obstacles to Change in Latin America*. London: Oxford University Press.

Endah, Alberthiene. 2012. *Jokowi: Memimpin Kota, Menyentuh Jakarta*. Solo: Metagraf.

Erb, Meribeth, and Priyambudi Sulistiyanto, eds. 2009. *Deepening Democracy in Indonesia? Direct Elections for Local Leaders (Pilkada)*. Singapore: ISEAS.

Fealy, Greg. 2011. "Indonesian Politics in 2011: Democratic Regression and Yudhoyono's Regal Incumbency." *Bulletin of Indonesian Economic Studies* 47 (3): 333–353.

———. 2015. "The Politics of Yudhoyono: Majoritarian Democracy, Insecurity and Vanity." In Aspinall, Edward, Marcus Mietzner, and Dirk Tomsa, eds. 2015. *The Yudhoyono Presidency: Indonesia's Decade of Stability and Stagnation*. Singapore: ISEAS.

Feith, Herbert. 1962. *The Decline of Constitutional Democracy in Indonesia*. Ithaca, New York: Cornell University Press.

Freedom House. 2006. *Freedom in the World 2006*. Washington, DC: Freedom House.

———. 2014. *Freedom in the World 2014*. Washington, DC: Freedom House.

Gammon, Liam. 2012. "Voters, Elites, and Urban Planning in an Asian Megacity: A Case Study of the 2012 Gubernatorial Elections in Jakarta." Honors Thesis, Australian National University.

———. 2014. "Jokowi the Party Man," *New Mandala*, April 1. http://asiapacific.anu. edu.au/newmandala/.

Hadiz, Vedi R. 2010. *Localising Power in Post-Authoritarian Indonesia: A Southeast Asia Perspective.* Stanford: Stanford University Press.

———. 2014. "The Dumbing Down of Indonesian Voters: A Scholar's View," Interview in *Magdalene*, June 13. www.magdalene.co.

Hadiz, Vedi R., and Richard Robison. 2014. "The Political Economy of Oligarchy and the Reorganization of Power in Indonesia." In Ford, Michele, and Thomas P. Pepinsky, eds. 2014. *Beyond Oligarchy: Wealth, Power and Contemporary Indonesian Politics.* Ithaca: Cornell Southeast Asia Program Publications.

Hamid, Abdul. 2014. "Jokowi's Populism in the 2012 Jakarta Gubernatorial Election." *Journal of Current Southeast Asian Affairs* 33 (1): 85–109.

Harsono, Andreas. 2014. "Voting Against Indonesia's Religious Intolerance." Human Rights Watch News, July 18. http://www.hrw.org/news.

Hawkins, Kirk. 2003. "Populism in Venezuela: The Rise of Chavismo." *Third World Quarterly* 24 (6): 1,137–1,160.

Hill, Hal. 2014. "A Development Policy Agenda for a New Administration." *Inside Indonesia* 117, July–September.

Howes, Stephen, and Robin Davies. 2014. "Survey of Recent Developments." *Bulletin of Indonesian Economic Studies* 50 (2): 157–83.

Indikator Politik. 2014. *Hasil Exit Poll Pemilu Presiden RI 2014, Rabu, 9 Juli 2014.* Indikator Politik, Jakarta.

Indo Barometer. 2014. *The Final Round: Siapakah Pemenang Pilpres 9 Juli 2014?* Indo Barometer, Jakarta. www.indobarometer.com.

Katz, Richard S., and Peter Mair. 1995. "Changing Models of Party Organization and Party Democracy: The Emergence of the Cartel Party." *Party Politics* 1 (1): 5–28.

———. 1996. "Cadre, Catch-All or Cartel? A Rejoinder." *Party Politics* 2 (4): 525–34.

———. 2009. "The Cartel Party Thesis: A Restatement." *Perspectives on Politics* 7 (4): 753–66.

———. 2012. "Parties, Interest Groups and Cartels: A Comment." *Party Politics* 18 (1): 107–11.

Kosuke, Mizuno, and Pasuk Phongpaichit, eds. 2009. *Populism in Asia.* Singapore: NUS Press.

Lee, Terence. 2013. "Legacies of Authoritarian Rule: Retired Officers and Elections in Indonesia." Paper presented at the Inter-University Seminar on *Armed Forces and Society* Biennial Convention Chicago, October.

Levitsky, Steven, and James Loxton. 2013. "Populism and Competitive Authoritarianism in the Andes." *Democratization* 20 (1): 107–136.

Liddle, R. William. 2014. "Improving the Quality of Democracy in Indonesia: Toward a Theory of Action." In Ford, Michele, and Thomas P. Pepinsky, eds. 2014. *Beyond Oligarchy: Wealth, Power and Contemporary Indonesian Politics.* Ithaca: Cornell Southeast Asia Program Publications.

Lorenz, Philip. 2013. "Patronage, Personalismus, Professionalisierung: Die vorsichtige Demokratisierung zivil-militärischer Beziehungen in Indonesien." Frankfurt am Main: Hessische Stiftung für Friedens- und Konfliktforschung.

McCargo, Duncan, and Ukrist Pathmanand. 2005. *The Thaksinization of Thailand.* Copenhagen: NIAS Press.

McVey, Henry H. 2013. "Indonesia: Transitioning Potential into Reality." 3(5). New York: KKR Global Perspectives, June.

Mietzner, Marcus. 2005. "Local Democracy." *Inside Indonesia* 85, January–March.

———. 2009. *Military Politics, Islam and the State in Indonesia: From Turbulent Transition to Democratic Consolidation.* Singapore: ISEAS.

———. 2012a. "Indonesia's Democratic Stagnation: Anti-Reformist Elites and Resilient Civil Society." *Democractization* 19 (2): 209–29.

———. 2012b. "Ideology, Money and Dynastic Leadership: The Indonesian Democratic Party of Struggle, 1998-2012." *South East Asian Research* 20 (4): 511–31.

———. 2013. "Fighting the Hellhounds: Pro-democracy Activists and Party Politics in Post-Suharto Indonesia." *Journal of Contemporary Asia* 43 (1): 28–50.

———. 2014a. "The President, the "Deep State" and Policymaking in Post-Suharto Indonesia: A Case Study of the Deliberations on the Civil Service Act." Report for the Partnership on Governance Reform (Kemitraan), Jakarta.

———. 2014b. "Jokowi: Rise of a Polite Populist," *Inside Indonesia* 116, April–June.

———. 2014c. "Indonesia's 2014 Elections: How Jokowi Won and Democracy Survived." *Journal of Democracy* 25 (4): 111–25.

Morfit, Michael. 2007. "The Road to Helsinki: The Aceh Agreement and Indonesia's Democratic Development." *International Negotiation* 12 (1): 111–43.

Oberman, Raoul, et al. 2012. *The Archipelago Economy: Unleashing Indonesia's Potential.* Seoul and Washington, DC: McKinsey Global Institute.

Pappas, Takis S. 2014. *Populism and Crisis Politics in Greece.* London: Palgrave McMillan.

Pappas, Takis S., and Hanspeter Kriesi, 2015. "Populism and Crisis: A Fuzzy Relationship." In Kriesi, Hanspeter, and Takis S. Pappas, eds. 2015. *European Populism in the Shadow of the Great Recession.* Essex: ECPR.

Purdey, Emma. 2014. "The Myth and Making of a Political Dynasty." Melbourne University Election Watch Indonesia, July 4. http://electionwatch.edu.au/ indonesia-2014/myth-and-making-political-dynasty.

Reid, Anthony, ed. 2012. *Indonesia Rising: The Repositioning of Asia's Third Giant.* Singapore: ISEAS.

Roberts, K.M. 2000. "Populism and Democracy in Latin America." Lecture at Carter Center, Atlanta. www.cartercenter.org/documents/nondatabase/roberts.pdf.

Sherlock, Stephen. 2015. "The Presidency and Inter-Institutional Relations under Yudhoyono." In Aspinall, Edward, Marcus Mietzner, and Dirk Tomsa, eds. 2015. *The Yudhoyono Presidency: Indonesia's Decade of Stability and Stagnation.* Singapore: ISEAS.

Slater, Dan. 2004. "Indonesia's Accountability Trap: Party Cartels and Presidential Power after Democratic Transition." *Indonesia* 78: 61–92.

———. 2011. "Unbuilding Blocs: Cleavages and Cartelization in Indonesian Party Politics, 1999–2009." Paper presented at workshop on "Political Articulation," Chicago, April.

———. 2014. "Promiscuity into Promise?" *New Mandala*, June 2. http://asiapacific. anu.edu.au/newmandala/.

Slater, Dan, and Erica Simmons. 2013. "Coping by Colluding: Political Uncertainty and Promiscuous Powersharing in Indonesia and Bolivia." *Comparative Political Studies* 46 (12): 1,366–1,393.

SMRC - Saiful Mujani Research and Consulting. 2014a. *Koalisi untuk Calon Presiden: Elite vs. Massa Pemilih Partai, Temuan Survei: 20 – 24 April 2014.* Jakarta: SMRC.

———2014b. *Survei Nasional Pemilihan Presiden- Wakil Presiden, 30 Juni – 3 Juli 2014.* Jakarta: SMRC.

———2014c. *Kinerja Demokrasi dan Pilpres 2014: Evaluasi Pemilih Nasional, Temuan Survei: 21–26 Juli 2014.* Jakarta: SMRC.

Suaedy, Ahmad. 2014. "The Role of Volunteers and Political Participation in the 2012 Jakarta Gubernatorial Election." *Journal of Current Southeast Asian Affairs* 33 (1): 111–138.

Tapsell, Ross, and Liam Gammon. 2014. "Field Notes on the Jokowi Campaign," *New Mandala*, July 4. http://asiapacific.anu.edu.au/newmandala/.

Tomsa, Dirk. 2009. "The Eagle Has Crash-landed," *Inside Indonesia* 97, July–September.

———. 2010. "Indonesian Politics in 2010: The Perils of Stagnation." *Bulletin of Indonesian Economic Studies* 46 (3): 309–328.

Torre, Carlos de la. 2013. "Latin America's Authoritarian Drift: Technocratic Populism in Ecuador." *Journal of Democracy* 24 (3): 33–46.

Varshney, Ashutosh. 2014. "Hindu Nationalism in Power?" *Journal of Democracy* 25 (4): 34–45.

von Luebke, Christian. 2014 "Maverick Mayor to Presidential Hopeful," *Inside Indonesia* 115, January–March.

Winters, Jeffrey A. 2011. " Who Will Tame the Oligarchs?" *Inside Indonesia* 104, April–June.

———. 2013. "Oligarchy and Democracy in Indonesia." *Indonesia* 96: 11–33.

World Bank. 2014a. "Manufacturing, Value Added (% of GDP)." http://data.worldbank.org/indicator/NV.IND.MANF.ZS.

———. 2014b. "Poverty Headcount Ratio at $2 a Day (PPP) (% of population)." http://data.worldbank.org/indicator/SI.POV.2DAY.

———. 2014c. "Health Expenditure, Total (% of GDP)." http://data.worldbank.org/indicator/SH.XPD.TOTL.ZS.

———. 2014d. "Public Spending on Education, Total (% of GDP)." http://data.worldbank.org/indicator/SE.XPD.TOTL.GD.ZS.

Yudhoyono, Susilo Bambang. 2014. *Selalu Ada Pilihan: Untuk Pencinta Demokrasi dan Para Pemimpin Indonesia Mendatang.* Jakarta: Kompas.

www.ingramcontent.com/pod-product-compliance
Lightning Source LLC
Chambersburg PA
CBHW050554280326
41933CB00011B/1834